VILLAGE
INDIA

STEPHEN P. HUYLER

VILLAGE INDIA

HARRY N. ABRAMS, INC., PUBLISHERS, NEW YORK

Editor: Sheila Franklin
Designer: Tina Davis Snyder

Page 6: A Rajput woman adorned in her silver and gold dowry sits in the
stone parapet of her house in Pushkar, Ajmer District, Rajasthan.

Library of Congress Cataloging in Publication Data

Huyler, Stephen.
  Village India.

  Bibliography: p.
  Includes index.
  1. India—Description and travel—1981-
2. Villages—India. 3. India—Rural conditions.
I. Title.
DS414.2.H88 1985 306'.0954 85-1271
ISBN 0-8109-1728-9

Photographs by Stephen P. Huyler copyright © 1985 Stephen P. Huyler

Map by Joseph E. Schwartzberg and Philip A. Schwartzberg

Published in 1985 by Harry N. Abrams, Incorporated, New York
All rights reserved. No part of the contents of this book may be
reproduced without the written permission of the publishers

Printed and bound in Japan

To Helene, my wife,
without whose constant love and support my work would not have been possible

CONTENTS

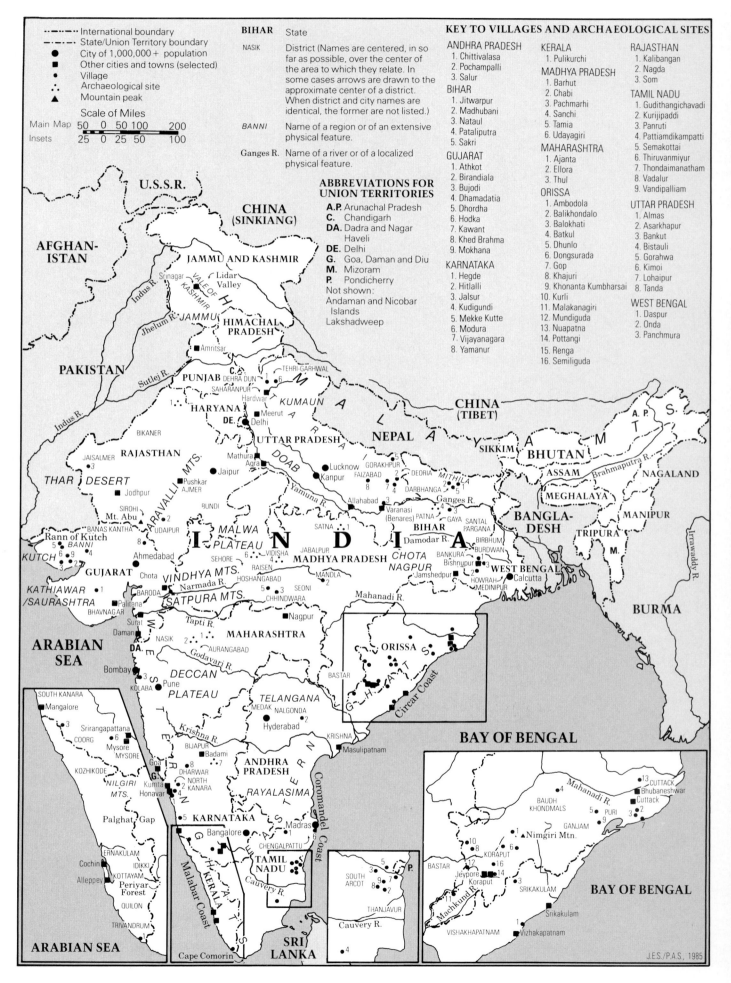

International boundary
State/Union Territory boundary
● City of 1,000,000 + population
■ Other cities and towns (selected)
∴ Village
∴ Archaeological site
▲ Mountain peak

Scale of Miles
Main Map 50 0 50 100   200
Insets   25 0 25 50   100

BIHAR   State

NASIK   District (Names are centered, in so
           far as possible, over the center of
           the area to which they relate. In
           some cases arrows are drawn to the
           approximate center of a district.
           When district and city names are
           identical, the former are not listed.)

BANNI   Name of a region or of an extensive
           physical feature.

Ganges R. Name of a river or of a localized
           physical feature.

ABBREVIATIONS FOR
UNION TERRITORIES
A.P. Arunachal Pradesh
C.   Chandigarh
DA. Dadra and Nagar
     Haveli
DE. Delhi
G.   Goa, Daman and Diu
M.   Mizoram
P.   Pondicherry
Not shown:
Andaman and Nicobar
   Islands
Lakshadweep

KEY TO VILLAGES AND ARCHAEOLOGICAL SITES

ANDHRA PRADESH
1. Chittivalasa
2. Pochampalli
3. Salur
BIHAR
1. Jitwarpur
2. Madhubani
3. Nataul
4. Pataliputra
5. Sakri
GUJARAT
1. Athkot
2. Birandiala
3. Bujodi
4. Dhamadatia
5. Dhordha
6. Hodka
7. Kawant
8. Khed Brahma
9. Mokhana
KARNATAKA
1. Hegde
2. Hitlalli
3. Jalsur
4. Kudigundi
5. Mekke Kutte
6. Modura
7. Vijayanagara
8. Yamanur

KERALA
1. Pulikurchi
MADHYA PRADESH
1. Barhut
2. Chabi
3. Pachmarhi
4. Sanchi
5. Tamia
6. Udayagiri
MAHARASHTRA
1. Ajanta
2. Ellora
3. Thul
ORISSA
1. Ambodola
2. Balikhondalo
3. Balokhati
4. Batkul
5. Dhunlo
6. Dongsurada
7. Gop
8. Khajuri
9. Khonanta Kumbharsai
10. Kurli
11. Malakanagiri
12. Mundiguda
13. Nuapatna
14. Pottangi
15. Renga
16. Semiliguda

RAJASTHAN
1. Kalibangan
2. Nagda
3. Som
TAMIL NADU
1. Gudithangichavadi
2. Kurijipaddi
3. Panruti
4. Pattiamdikampatti
5. Semakottai
6. Thiruvanmiyur
7. Thondaimanatham
8. Vadalur
9. Vandipalliam
UTTAR PRADESH
1. Almas
2. Asarkhapur
3. Bankut
4. Bistauli
5. Gorahwa
6. Kimoi
7. Lohaipur
8. Tanda
WEST BENGAL
1. Daspur
2. Onda
3. Panchmura

J.E.S./P.A.S., 1985

ACKNOWLEDGMENTS

I have received so much help in my years of research that it would be impossible to give credit to all. First I would like to thank Beatrice Wood for suggesting this research in the first place and for encouraging it at every stage. Through her, I met two great Indian women, Rukmini Devi Arundale and Kamala Devi Chattopadhyaya, both leaders in the movement to protect Indian art and craft traditions. With their introductions, I have met sympathetic Indians wherever I have traveled.

I am grateful to my parents for their encouragement, and particularly to my father for his help in editing this manuscript; to my uncle, Coulter D. Huyler, for his rare understanding; to Mr. and Mrs. C. S. Wheeler III for their understanding support; to Reginald and Gladys Laubin for their inspiration; to Andrée Schlemmer for the perspective and motivations she provided; to my mentors at the University of Denver: Dr. Charles Geddes, Mary C. Lanius, Dr. Kate Kent, and Dr. James Kirk; and at London University's School of Oriental and African Studies: Dr. John Burton-Page. In London the late Bill Archer gave me invaluable help and insight into my work. I would also like to thank my colleagues Steven J. Cohen and Dr. Heather Marshall; and those who have kindly contributed their photographs and advice to this book: John M. Silverstein, Stella Snead, Bill and Katherine Hacker, Dr. Ronald M. Bernier, Michael Head, Dr. Jyotindra Jain, Dr. George Michell, and, again, Mary Lanius and my father, John S. Huyler III. I would also like to thank those people I have worked with at Harry N. Abrams: Paul Gottlieb for his initial interest and foresight; Barbara Lyons for her help in selecting photographs; Tina Davis Snyder for her thoughtful approach to layout and design; and, especially, my editor, Sheila Franklin, for her sensitivity and perception at every stage.

This book is really dedicated to the peoples of India whose hospitality, thoughtfulness, warmth, and encouragement have made me feel at home and at ease wherever I have traveled. I have met with fine scholars throughout the subcontinent, who have given freely of their time and information to provide me with a basis for understanding rural India. In villages, towns, and cities everywhere people have helped me, fed me, and let me enter their lives. I cannot possibly name them all, but to them I am forever grateful. Of those who have been especially helpful, I would like to thank Diwan Sham Lal Sawhney of New Delhi, and particularly his late wife, Teni Sen Sawhney; Air Marshall G. B. Singh of New Delhi; the family of K. K. Pillai of Hyderabad; D. G. Kelkar of Pune; N. T. Vakani of Ahmedabad; Anand and Kalyan Krishna and P. P. Tewari of Varanasi; the late Vaithyalinga Pathar, and his wife, Amma, of Gudithangichavadi, South Arcot District, Tamil Nadu; Shiva Kumar of Madras; Rukmini Devi, Shankara Menon, Kamala Trilokekar, Padmasini, and Peter and Sharada Hoffman of Kalakshetra; Govind Swamy Naidu of Mysore; Sitakant Mahapatra, I. C. S. of Bhubaneshwar; and A. K. Mohanty and members of the Tribal and Harijan Research and Training Institute, Bhubaneshwar. Without their interest, understanding, and inspiration my travels and research in India would have been far more difficult.

Stephen P. Huyler

9

PREFACE

This monumental sculpture of Nandi, the bull mount of Shiva, was carved from a single boulder in 1664 and stands near Mysore, Karnataka. Pilgrims come from all over India to make offerings before the image, which symbolizes fertility and strength.

A seventh of the world's population, more than 615 million people, live in India's villages, yet few people outside of India know much about them. Writers and filmmakers tend to emphasize the classical courts, various imperial powers, religious ascetics or cult groups, and the poverty- or disaster-stricken. Each of these is a minority. India embraces more diversity of culture than does any other similar landmass in the world, but in proportion to the full population, these factions are only a small percentage, worthy of note, but not to the exclusion of the majority. The aim of this book is to dispel many Western misconceptions about India and to portray that subcontinent as it is: largely rural, beautiful in its complexity, and rich in both customs and creativity.

India, by Western standards, is an impoverished country. But the image that most Westerners have of it as hopelessly retrograde is inaccurate, fostered largely by media that exaggerate the negative conditions, while ignoring the broader context in which they occur. I have not found poverty everywhere I travel in India, and certainly have not found widespread despair. The worst conditions exist in isolated pockets, particularly in the northeast, and are generally the result of overpopulation or physical disasters such as hurricanes or droughts. I have included a history section in my text, largely to provide a broader framework: to show the development of Indian villages and the ways in which they have influenced the evolution of Western history from the time of the Greeks and Romans to the present, as well as to portray the reasons for the contemporary difficulties existing in rural

India and the solutions being adopted by modern India in an attempt to cope with those difficulties.

I consider myself an ethnologist in the process of conducting a lifelong cross-cultural survey of Indian villages. The focus of my work is the study of traditional rural material culture; that is, of all the material apects of a village (its arts, crafts, architecture, and tools, to name only a few). A society's material culture is a direct reflection of its peoples; in order to understand it, one must have as broad a knowledge as possible of all the factors that went into its creation and use (of environmental statistics, technical data, history, religion, sociology, and folklore). This book is a natural outgrowth of my research, which, so far, has entailed extensive, regular travel in India during the past fourteen years. In that time I have covered much of the subcontinent, but not all. The material which follows is selected from those areas in which I have worked myself, and is derived primarily from the villages of twelve states, which together comprise most of the Indian subcontinent. (The states not included are Himachal Pradesh, Punjab, Haryana, Sikkim, Assam, Meghalaya, Tripura, Manipur, and Nagaland.) I have not attempted a comprehensive survey of each state, but rather, in the description of each have used local examples to highlight certain facets of the broader Indian rural culture. My research has been almost entirely in Hindu villages (eighty-four percent of India's population is Hindu), with the exception of two years spent working among the tribal peoples of central India, primarily in Orissa. Although many religious minorities exist in India, this book focuses on Hindu and tribal cultures.

Stripes have been painted on these simple mud walls to enhance their appearance. (Yamanur, Karnataka)

The selected photographs are by nature subjective, portraying some of the diversity I have seen in my travels. The images they record are by no means exceptional, but are representative of village life generally, caught at a moment when the use of a camera was not disruptive. The richness of the culture is such that, although the character of villages and people changes dramatically from one region to the next, almost any group of villages in India would afford a similar wealth of imagery.

When I first traveled in India, I went by local transport as much as possible: by train, bus, boat, and cart. In order to reach difficult areas more easily, I now usually travel by car or jeep. When possible I stay in small hotels or government guest houses. Otherwise, as people in Indian villages are extremely hospitable, I stay as their guest in village homes. Since few people travel to these villages, and as few outsiders have cared to document rural material culture, I am encouraged and helped wherever I go. I eat local food and, when it seems clean, drink local water. As a tall white foreigner in areas that rarely, if ever, see outsiders, it is difficult to be inconspicuous. There are no social mores in India prohibiting staring and the asking of personal questions, and any stranger is fair game. Everywhere I go I am asked by villagers how much money I make, how much my clothes or camera cost, and for the most intimate details of my private life. As much as possible, however, I try to keep a low profile and to document rural material culture in its natural state. Long ago, I learned that taking photographs is, in a way, like taking a gift from the subject, so I now bring with me almost as much Polaroid film as 35mm film, and

when I take a picture, I give one in return. Languages and dialects often change from one area to the next. Although not a linguist, I try to familiarize myself with the major languages of a state in which I am working and find communicating with signs easy. Usually I can find someone, even in remote villages, who speaks English, the traditional language of administration in India.

India has given me so much during my years of travel and study—a richness and wealth of experience I could never have imagined fourteen years ago, when I first traveled there. In the West I am constantly asked by people how I can stomach India's oppressive social strictures and impoverished living conditions. But these things have little to do with my experience of the country. Wherever I travel in India I am met with warmth and thoughtfulness, with interest in and encouragement of my work— with such positive human response. In the West the comprehensiveness of our media coverage leads us to believe that every corner of our world has been explored, every discipline documented, yet rural India presents a frontier for discovery. The changes, both subtle and dramatic, from village to village and state to state are fascinating, aspects so little recorded that my life as a researcher is filled with a seeming infinity of choices, all stimulating and rewarding. In the following pages, I hope to share with the reader some of the splendid diversity I have found in my travels throughout rural India and, in doing so, to encourage a reevaluation and further exploration of what is truly an astounding subcontinent.

13

PROLOGUE

The layout of streets and houses varies in each area. In the villages of Uttar Pradesh, streets are irregular, unordered, and intersected by blind alleys. Women in this state are not as evident in public as they are farther east or in the south. Most do not work in the fields, vend in markets, or congregate in the streets. *Saris* are drawn over the head, and faces are covered in front of strangers. (Varanasi District)

Nothing marks the turn to the village: no signs, shops, or houses. We have been told that it lies "several furlongs" from the main road, but that, in India, can mean anything from a few hundred yards to a few miles. The road is dusty and deeply rutted, occasionally bordered by mango trees. The only vehicle we meet is a wooden-wheeled cart piled high with sugarcane and pulled slowly by a lone bullock. Short, straight mounds of earth begin to divide the flat expanse of the landscape into geometric patterns of green and brown. A band of tall sugarcane fringed by coconut palms defines the horizon, while in the foreground the vibrant green is cut by a line of moving vermilion: women in bright *saris*, bent at the waist, legs straight, planting rice. The few scattered farmhouses with mud walls and roofs of buff tile seem almost to blend into the fields, accented only by a few banana and papaya trees, one house with a large melon vine growing on its roof. The air is clean and quiet, except for the distant, high-pitched sounds of the women singing as they plant, the creaking of a large wooden mill being pulled to grind by two water buffalo, and the ubiquitous cawing of the Indian crows.

We are aware of the village long before we come to it. On the left, just off the road, is a small pond, its surface covered with lotuses and water hyacinths. To one edge of the pond is a glade of trees and scrub brush grouped around an ancient, gnarly tree. A large stone blackened with oil and streaked with bright red sits directly beneath this tree, a garland of marigolds coiled at its base. Around it are placed several stylized clay figures of horses. The stone, although shapeless, is the primordial image of the local god of protection for the village and for the crops. He has probably been worshiped in this stone form for a thousand years, perhaps much longer. The horses are given as mounts for him to ride at night in defense of his devotees. A passing farmer, head bent and palms pressed together in reverence, places a hibiscus flower in front of the stone before continuing to his fields.

Ahead the village is marked by a broad group of trees, mostly palms, with a hill of jagged boulders standing directly behind them. As we enter, our senses are struck by colors, textures, sounds, rhythms, and smells, each demanding immediate notice, but each overlaid and infused with one another. A step into an Indian village challenges all one's attention and emotions.

We are immediately surrounded by all the village's unoccupied inhabitants, a sea of faces questioning and staring. Who are we? Where are we from? Why are we here? There are no shops, general provisions stores, restaurants, cafes, or tea shops, but the village is very active. The farmers who are at home are sorting produce, repairing tools, and harnessing their bullocks; craftsmen, each within his own compound, are plying their trades; women are cleaning their homes, preparing and cooking food, and carrying water; children are either in school or busy at their daily chores. Villagers are friendly; it is an honor in India to be a host, so that as we walk down the street, we are continually asked to visit homes, to have a cup of tea, some coconut water, some food. Visually, the village is both simple and ornate. The houses of smooth mud walls roofed with locally fired tiles, each with a

15

In Madhya Pradesh houses generally comprise three or four rectangular rooms built around a courtyard. Walls are made of rammed earth and support slanted roofs of locally made flat tiles. In most seasons women cook in the courtyard; when it rains, they move inside, the smoke from their fires drifting up through holes in the roof, which have been covered over with raised tiles to keep out the rain. (Udayagiri, Vidisha District)

Houses in a village in Puri District, Orissa, share common walls and are joined by a long narrow verandah. The mud walls have been decorated with rice-paste designs by the women of each household as a tribute to Lakshmi, the goddess of prosperity and protector of the home.

raised verandah at the front, give the street a clean and orderly appearance. The main street is aligned north to south, with several smaller streets and alleys set at right angles to it. The villagers, walking down the street, to and from their farms and various activities, peering out of doors, and grouped on verandahs trying to comprehend this apparition of foreigners within their community, are dressed in regional style. The women wear colorful cotton, and occasionally synthetic, *saris*; their necks and wrists are laden with silver and glass jewelry. Most of the men wear white and are in the traditional male dress, a long piece of cloth folded between the legs (a *dhoti*) surmounted by a long shirt and vest. Others wear the more contemporary costume of Western-cut trousers and shirts.

Voices are insistent and loud. Villages are always a mixture of intense noise and sublime quiet. We accept one invitation, step up onto a verandah, bend low to cross the threshold, and pass by a door carved with patterns of fishes and birds. On the street we were surrounded by all the village children and many adults. Inside there is only the family, although that is quite large, since most people in Indian villages still live in extended families, with the immediate members of the family as well as all the aunts, uncles, and cousins related to the male line living under the same roof. The eldest male is in charge of the entire family, its movements and activities, his wife running the household. Both are held in great respect. Meals are communal, although each dependent family usually has its own sleeping quarters. We enter the house through a main room, which in the rainy season is used for

gathering, cooking, and eating as well as for sleeping by some of the family. Behind this room is a courtyard, with several sleeping and storage rooms radiating from it. The courtyard is the center of activity in this, the dry season. Completely protected from the outside, it is quiet. The smells strike us first: spicy vegetables simmering in a large brass pot over a simple clay stove fueled by cow dung mixed with straw. While tending the pot, an old aunt rolls dough into flat cakes on a smooth stone. An elder daughter is laying out red chili peppers fresh from the field to dry in the sun. Another girl scrubs out a blackened brass pan over a drain in the corner, periodically splashing water into it from a clay pot. This is a family of farmers, as are most in this village of 982 people. Using a simple wooden plow drawn by water buffalo, these farmers work hard to make their few acres of land produce enough rice, millet, and sugarcane for themselves and, it is hoped, for others to buy at the weekly market. Today, most of the men are out working in the fields, but a rheumatic grandfather is sitting on a step in front of one of the rooms. We are asked to sit in the shade of the overhanging eaves and wait for tea to be made.

The walls of the courtyard are adorned with white rice-paste designs in the form of flowers and animals. These were recently painted by the family's women for a festival honoring the goddess of the home. Each room and the courtyard itself, all with plain mud floors, are impeccably clean, simply designed, and furnished with economy of space in mind. In the rooms sleeping mats and quilts are rolled up and placed in a corner, and wooden beams

Each village or group of villages has developed its own style of craftsmanship. One may be well known for its pottery, another for its brassmaking, and yet another for its jewelry. In the village of Asarkhapur in Gorakhpur District, Uttar Pradesh, Harijan (Untouchable) girls weave colorful baskets to be sold to villagers in the local market.

bination of wood, cow dung, and precious coal, is kept red-hot by a huge animal-headed bellows, which is manipulated by the brazier's two small sons. The craftsman pulls from the fire a piece of molten brass, and his two brothers alternately pound it flat with large hammers. After this flattened plate has cooled, the brazier then beats and shapes it to form the sides of a large water pot, adding a circular base and brazing the seams. He also makes a variety of cooking pots and utensils as well as some religious paraphernalia, most of which he sells directly to a trader who, in turn, hawks it at the weekly market.

Also on this street live two weaver families. One of the weavers' wives has brought out her small children to the front verandah to meet us, and we learn, in talking with her, that all the men in both families are away. Some are irrigating the rice in their small plot beyond the village, but her husband, along with several other men from both families, has had to take a job in a town factory more than a hundred miles away. He is able to visit her only occasionally, and then just for a day at a time, but he regularly sends her small amounts of money. The traditional weaving of this village is no longer in frequent demand, and for most of the year, except in the wet monsoon season when farming is impossible, the simple wooden looms are kept stored on the rafters above the sleeping rooms. The weaving of handspun, vegetable-dyed cotton *saris* for women and plain white *dhotis* for men provided a steady and respectable living for the ancestors of these people, but with the advent of inexpensive modern machine textiles and government-subsidized

handwoven cloth from other villages, the need for this profession locally has all but disappeared. As we sit talking to this woman, her son brings us green coconuts, the tops of which he cuts off with a large machete-like knife, and we drink their sweet, refreshing liquid. Villagers in India, no matter how poor they are, always offer guests food, and it is considered ungracious and insulting to refuse. While we are drinking the coconut water, an old woman comes by, carrying on her head a large basket full of smaller baskets, pots, and cloth bundles. She is the village grocery vendor, who travels from house to house here and in neighboring villages selling vegetables, salt, spices, and other staples. In her high, cracked voice she describes each of her goods to the weaver's wife, who rarely has enough money to buy them. When we leave a short while later, the old vendor is engrossed in relating all the village gossip. There are no local newspapers here, but the villagers keep informed through sources such as the vegetable vendor; the village Brahmans, who read one of the city papers; and the local politicians, who canvas the area frequently. Decisions about local concerns are decided by a village-elected body of men, mostly elders, while elections are regularly held to fill district, state, and national offices. India is the world's largest democracy, and although pressure is sometimes brought to bear on villagers to vote for a certain candidate or party, elections are for the most part free.

Back on the main street, we pass by many more farmers' houses similar to the first one we entered. Our movements draw behind us a crowd of villagers, mostly children, wherever we go. The simple, smoothed mud of the houses is broken in a few places by roughly painted words and symbols in black and red: party slogans demanding a vote. A single wire runs along the rooftops feeding some of the houses with electricity, introduced to the village eight years ago. Those who have the current usually use it to power only a single lightbulb in their courtyards.

On the right towards the end of the street is a compound with a high brick wall. This is the home of the local Brahmans. The house inside this lot is much more modern than the others in the village, a perfect square in design, built of brick and some cement along with the traditional mud. The members of this family are the largest landowners in the village, and although they do not farm the land themselves (hiring others to do that work), they serve the village as both priests and teachers. They are by no means wealthy, but compared to the rest of the villagers, they are comfortable. In times of crisis, however, such as droughts or hurricanes, they, too, become impoverished. In a corner of the Brahmans' compound is a small white shrine built of plastered brick. This shrine contains the personal gods of the family, small brass images of Vishnu and Lakshmi, the goddess of home and fortune, perhaps made in the last century by an ancestor of the brazier. The statues are clothed in red and gold silk, with garlands of drying marigolds surrounding them. In front of them lie two black fossilized shells, or *salagramas*, symbols of Vishnu, and a small brass dish lamp. The sides and back of the shrine are blackened with smoke and covered with the small stick remnants of incense. The eldest

Brahman and his family worship at this shrine every morning before breakfast and every evening before dinner.

Just past the Brahmans' compound we come to a huge banyan tree, which covers an enormous area, its roots hanging like snakes from its branches. Our attention is momentarily diverted from it by loud, thumping sounds echoing down the street. Beyond the tree is a small river, edged on the street side with a series of ancient, irregular stone steps. The noise is caused by several women, up to their knees in the water, their bright cotton *saris* tucked high onto their thighs, busily at work pounding wet laundry against the rocks. This is the traditional way of washing clothes in India, using muscle and sand instead of soap. Much earlier in the day, the river was the source of another type of activity: prayer. Before dawn, most of the villagers are awake, the women often rising at four o'clock to begin preparing the day's food. Upon waking, each villager, male and female, clears his throat and nostrils and then brushes his teeth with the bitter twig of the margosa tree, known for its medicinal properties. Then, before eating, each goes to the river to bathe in order to cleanse himself of the previous day's impurities. While standing in the water in his wet clothes he begins his prayers by directing his thoughts to the new day's sun. He then goes to the riverbank and changes into a fresh cloth adroitly, with the utmost modesty. As he returns to his home, he may stop at the small stone temple nearby, underneath the banyan tree, to give an offering of fruit or flowers to the gods. He is then free to have his first food and to begin his day's work.

The stone temple, unremarkable in its architecture, was probably built between the twelfth and the fourteenth centuries. The banyan tree's branches provide shelter for most of the uneven stone courtyard, the dangling roots trimmed like curtains to frame the shrine. In the center of the shrine is an old stone sculpture of Vishnu, its features coarse and almost worn away. Equally old sculptures of Vishnu's consorts, Shri Devi and Bhu Devi, occupy their own niches, and a blackened statue of Hanuman is placed outside the building at the base of one of the trunks of the banyan tree. The old Brahman spends most of his day here, tending to the images and the temple and conversing with all those who come by. In the early morning, after bathing and attending to his own shrine at home, this old man and his son come to the temple to prepare the images for worship. Through prayer and a series of prescribed rituals the energy of the deity, which is believed to be everywhere, is concentrated and awakened in the stone. Each statue is first bathed in water and then in oil and in clarified butter called *ghee*, and dots of sandalwood paste and vermilion are placed on its *chakras*, those parts of the image deemed to be symbolic centers of sacred energy. The images are then dressed in silk and adorned with flowers, after which a bell is rung, camphor incense lit, and a dish of bananas, coconuts, and more flowers placed before the deities in offering. During this entire ceremony, both priests have been loudly chanting prayers in Sanskrit. Finally, after a brass pan with several lighted wicks on it has been passed over each god to the accompaniment of clanging bells, the images are

Water is often the most important asset of an Indian village. Throughout the subcontinent, villages retain their water in reservoirs, called tanks, which are fed either by streams or by rainwater. Tanks provide water for irrigation and for drinking and are often used as a place to water livestock and wash clothes. At a tank's edge in Badami, Bijapur District, Karnataka, village women wash their families' clothes in the traditional fashion by beating them against stones. In most areas, soap is never used.

ready to be worshiped by the public.

On the other side of the banyan tree, outside the temple, a group of children is sitting on the ground at the feet of another Brahman, the old man's nephew. This is a traditional village primary school, where simple religious texts and elementary arithmetic and writing are taught. Apparently our arrival in the village had interrupted the instruction of the children. Now all are back, singing in unison their day's lesson, their shrill voices mixed with the steady percussion caused by the clothes washing. Unlike most of the other adults in the village, who are content with their own dialect, the Brahmans speak some English, the language of administration in India. As a sign of progress the teacher proudly has his class sing for us an old English nursery rhyme. Children are the focus of Indian village life and are treated with respect, responsibility, and humor. Prior to Indian independence in 1947, the village school was restricted to children from higher castes. Now, by law, any village children may attend, and classes are full. The Brahman children and a few children of the more successful farmers have gone on to study at higher levels in town, a long walk and bus ride away.

In order to have a broad view of the village, we decide to climb the hill rising behind the temple. As we pick our way up a path between sandstone boulders the size of cars, we come upon the ruins of another temple, partly set into a cave in a cliff. The columns of this temple were carved out of the solid rock of the hill, though some of its structure is of freestanding blocks. Although probably not recorded on any archaeological maps, it is clearly

The classes of rural Indian schools are frequently held outside. Here, the students of a dance and music school sit beneath a giant banyan tree reciting their morning prayers before class. (Kalakshetra in Thiruvanmiyur, Chengalpattu, Tamil Nadu)

over a thousand years old. The area is grown over with brush but the well-used path suggests frequent visitors. As we climb into the temple, we marvel at its strength and simplicity of design. We are startled to meet a middle-aged man, dressed in faded saffron clothes, with matted hair and white lines painted on his forehead. We have interrupted him eating cold rice out of a small brass pot. He is a *sadhu*, a holy man whose life is spent wandering all over India, who had come to the village some months before and decided to stay for a time. This temple, although no longer sanctified, its image long since missing, had originally been dedicated to Shiva, the god of creation and destruction. The *sadhu* is a devotee of Shiva, and has found this spot peaceful and conducive to his meditations. Early every day, after his ritual washing in the river, he goes throughout the neighboring villages chanting prayers and carrying his brass pot. By giving him food, perhaps some rice or yogurt, the villagers believe they will acquire merit with the gods.

Coming out of the cave temple, we notice a scraggly margosa tree to one side, its branches covered with small knotted strips of cloth. The *sadhu* explains that this tree is believed by the village women to be blessed by Mataji, the Supreme Mother. Barren women come here and tie cloth to the tree as part of a vow to the goddess, hoping that in return for their vow they will be given children.

Standing on a boulder next to this ancient temple, we look down on the village and the plain. The brown-red roofs of the houses, each framing a central courtyard, and the mud of the walls blending into the mud of the streets are juxtaposed to the

brilliant green of the rice paddies and sugarcane fields surrounding them. Down by the river, to our left, is the cremation ground, where the remains of each villager are reduced to ashes and offered to the god of the waters. To our right, at the opposite edge of the village, is a grove of trees reserved for market day, which once a week becomes the focus of all attention, of selling and buying, of gossip and storytelling, of yelling and laughter—a mass of color and movement. Traders come from the town and neighboring villages with a large variety of goods, farmers and craftsmen sell the products of their labor, and festivity abounds. Reflecting on our experiences in the village, we realize that despite the lack of modern plumbing and any machines, regardless of the little cement or whitewash, and the few new clothes, the villagers take great pride in the cleanliness of their streets, their homes, and themselves. Although the people are poor, we have not been aware of any extreme poverty or hunger here (something we have been led to expect but rarely find in Indian villages). The village is in harmony with its environment; people's lives are active and their traditions meaningful, and they seem content, even happy. As we stand on this rock, viewing the temples, the river, the village, and the farms, we are overwhelmed by a sense of timelessness.

ASPECTS OF
RURAL INDIA

Not all of India is densely populated. Throughout much of the country small villages nestle inconspicuously into the landscape, which varies greatly depending upon the region, containing such extremes as deserts and rainforests, arid plains and lush mountains, lowland alluvials and rocky plateaus. Here, in northern Karnataka, an ancient fortress dominates the cliffs that rise above the small town of Badami in Bijapur District.

Dense coconut groves interspersed with a variety of fruit trees cover the coastal lands of Kerala in the far south. Ancient inland waterways are still used as major trade routes, connecting isolated farmsteads and small villages with the outside world.

Villages are the repositories of culture in India, combinations of constancy and change. They are the root of all society, the common denominator in a country of diversity and contradiction. The first question an Indian asks a stranger is: "What is your village?" Most consider their ancestral villages their homes, even though their families may have lived for generations in cities.

India's size is only one third that of the continental United States, but its population is more than triple. Even so, density of population varies greatly from region to region, and many of India's five hundred thousand villages are set in open country with miles between settlements. Like the United States, India has no geographical standard. The South Asian subcontinent contains every extreme: the world's highest mountain range in the far north, one of the largest deserts in the world in its northwest, vast arid plains at its center, temperate mountain ranges along both the east and west coasts, and some of the most fertile, well-irrigated agricultural plains on earth in its north- and southeast. Its geography has divided it both internally and from the rest of the world, but its borders of mountains and seas have always challenged adventurers and conquerors, so that India has become a composite of different peoples and customs. Rainfall varies from as much as two hundred inches per annum in parts of the southwest (Karnataka) to as little as twelve inches in the northwest (Rajasthan). Seasonal winds, or monsoons, cause drastic changes in the weather—with intense heat offsetting torrential rains—and through the ages man has learned to adapt his agriculture and mode of life to accommodate and take advantage of them.

Rural India is equally diverse racially, although racial origins are in constant dispute. Each of the numerous large-scale immigrations to India, from early prehistoric times until the present day, has imparted its own racial characteristics. There is no norm. Some individual characteristics included within the Indian nation are features which may be described as Australoid or Negrito (short stature, very black skin, wide faces, and broad noses); Mongoloid (sturdy build, brown complexion, high cheekbones, and wide-spaced eyes with thick epicanthic folds); and Indo-European or -Aryan (tall, paler skin, lighter hair, and long heads with narrow features). This description is as inadequate as any brief classification of an extremely complex people must be, but it should serve to highlight some of the diversification that exists—a diversification that embraces not only northwestern Indians and Kashmiris, who could easily be mistaken for eastern Mediterraneans, but also central Indian tribal peoples, who closely resemble Africans. In general, the farther south one travels in India, the darker the people. Although the Indian ideal is to have fair skin (for example, families pray that their child will be born pale and try to arrange for fair-skinned brides for their sons), color does not seem to stigmatize in business or society. Socially, people are more concerned with geographic/ethnic origin and social position than they are with skin tone.

India is now divided into twenty-two states and nine union territories. With independence in 1947, the boundaries were formed according to major cultural divisions. Each kingdom or group of people

The tribal peoples of central India are relatively short in stature and have broad facial features somewhat similar to those of the South Sea islanders. The men of the Dongaria Kondh tribe, one of whom is shown here, wear their hair in buns, their bangs rolled back from their foreheads, and have pierced ears and noses. Although the author is one of the few outsiders ever to visit these people, they have nevertheless been exposed to certain Western influences. Young men typically wear Western-style shirts, which they buy in the weekly market. (Khajuri, Koraput District, Orissa)

The young Rajput men coming out of this house in Pushkar, Ajmer District, Rajasthan, have the fine facial features and tall stature typical of their caste. They wear traditional Rajput male attire: a *dhoti* wrapped tightly around the legs, a *kabja*, or tunic, buttoned up the front, and a brightly dyed *pagri*, or turban. Behind them wall paintings depict contemporary symbols of power: two guards, a car, a train, and an airplane.

Left: The dense rural population of Orissa in eastern India is not readily apparent to the visitor, for villages are often screened from view by plantations of coconut palms, bamboo, and mango trees. Lines of two and three houses, built of mud and dung strengthened with bamboo, are typically joined together, sharing common walls and verandahs, but maintaining separate interior courtyards. (Balikhondalo, Puri District)

Opposite: Rural Indians have traditionally adapted all available materials to practical uses within their villages. A superb contemporary example of this is suggested by the farmer's dwelling shown here, located near a factory that makes large ceramic electrical insulators. The farmer has ingeniously built the walls of his house out of salvaged broken insulators packed with mud, ensuring a sturdy structure and a cool interior in what is a particularly hot climate. (Vadalur, South Arcot District, Tamil Nadu)

in Indian history developed its own culture and usually its own language or dialect. The boundaries of these ancient kingdoms so often changed and overlaid one another throughout the centuries that each state contains many ethnic groups and dialects. Sanskrit is the root of most of the major languages in India, except for those of the south, which are Dravidian in origin. Derived from an Indo-Aryan base (from which English also evolved), Sanskrit, like its distant cousin Latin, is a language of ritual. Unlike Latin, it is a living language understood in varying degrees by millions throughout India. India has no common language, although the British insisted that English be the official language during their reign and educated peoples throughout the subcontinent still speak it. Since independence there has been continual pressure by the central govern-ment to adopt Hindi, a widespread indigenous language of northern India, as the lingua franca, but pressure from other vernacular areas, primarily from the south, has thwarted that attempt. There are twenty major languages in India, each with a different script (for example, every rupee has the amount printed on it in fourteen different scripts), and each is spoken by many millions of people. Aside from these broad-based languages, there are close to 150 more with fewer adherents, and of these languages many are further divided into several hundred dialects each. As dialects are frequently unintelligible from one group of villages to the next, many villagers speak more than one. Each specific dialect, with its unique oral history, helps to preserve the individual character and integrity of the rural society from which it comes. In a country as massive and complex as India, language helps to confirm a villager's identity.

Not surprisingly, given the numerous indigenous cultures and the varied topography, villages vary greatly in their composition. The Indian census considers a village to be any community with a population of less than five thousand. The number of inhabitants in many is actually under a thousand. In 1961 the population of the average Indian village was 635. A village is usually a cluster of dwellings in a geographically defined area, often with satellite hamlets for distinct social groups, such as craftsmen or Untouchables, surrounding it. The inhabitants are traditionally defined by their occupations, and each functions within an intricate system of interdependence. Often the majority of land surrounding a village is owned by the descendents of the community's founder, with land tenure a basis for most farming (usually the major occupation of the village). In states such as Kerala and West Bengal, where practical farming requires houses to be spread over a broad area, villages are more likely to be organized according to social rather than geographical considerations. Many new industrial cities in India are directly dependent upon the network of villages surrounding them for agricultural products. In addition to farmers, most villages or groups of villages within an accessible area have traditionally supported their own tradesmen and craftsmen (such as weavers, potters, carpenters, and metalsmiths) as well as providing for their own community services (such as sweeping and laundering).

A village may be defined by its own system of

local government, generally a community council of elected officials called a *panchayat*, or it may be organized solely for tax purposes as a means of creating revenue. In most cases officials elected to a *panchayat* are responsible for all matters concerning the community—things such as settling minor disputes and deciding local plans and actions. Problems concerning more than one village are brought before district officers, who work in conjunction with the state government and its officers. The latter are appointed through statewide elections. Aside from its own government officials each state capital is staffed with representatives of the central government in Delhi whose duties include informing the prime minister and Parliament of provincial conditions and implementing parliamentary measures. In the world's largest democracy, all villagers now technically have the right to direct representation at the district, state, and central government levels, but extreme bureaucracy and a long history of social strictures in regard to voting often impede the exercising of that right. The police are powerful in rural India, and although most villages are too small to have their own constabulary, they are usually protected and guarded by those of neighboring towns. (Remote villages tend to be relatively autonomous from the police.) Each town has a local jail, whose officers are responsible to the district headquarters, where there is a larger jail, and ultimately to the state capital and prison. The legal system in India is based upon the British model, with every man eligible for his own lawyer and a free trial, but in practice corruption is rife and the poor, lower-class villager has little hope of receiving a fair sentence.

A fundamental quality exhibited by Indians, both historically and today, is the ability to adapt and to encompass and utilize all available elements. The means of adaptation in India is very different from that which occurs in the West, where especially in America, attitudes change rapidly because of intense media exposure to new ideas. In India the very traditions themselves contain an integral adaptive mechanism for innovation. Indian villages express that adaptability through their extraordinary variety in form, content, and function. What seems to the outsider to be the epitome of the archaic settlement, unchanged through isolation, is in fact an epicenter of adjustment between tradition and innovation. The five thousand years of civilized development in India have seen innumerable influxes of immigrants and foreign travelers. Each has brought new ideas, technologies, and customs that have been absorbed by Indian culture. The majority of India has always been rural, not urban. Consequently, it is the villages which have borne this absorption. Their geographical extremes and relative isolation from one another have created unparalleled diversity, with each adapting uniquely to environment, indigenous materials, societal pressures, and historical and contemporary influences. As the environment itself rarely changes, regional adaptations often have the appearance of remaining fixed in form, with exterior influences assimilated only slowly. In the last hundred years, as conditions have worsened due to overpopulation and increased poverty, villagers have adapted by making use of all available elements.

Festivals provide villagers with a chance to put their work aside and forget their hardships. Pongal, celebrated throughout Tamil Nadu in January or February, is the most popular village festival. It lasts three days and culminates in the veneration of cattle as the symbol of all animals. *Top:* Cows are tied to the railing of a temporary enclosure where a Brahman priest, seated on a large ritual diagram, conducts prayers and blesses food. *Above:* The priest and a local female doctor prepare the food (bananas, special leaves and flowers, a type of rice candy, and a large pot of rice mixed with molasses), which will be fed to the cows, accompanied by words of praise and adoration, after it has been blessed. *Right:* A special cow at Pongal wears a crown of marigolds on her head, her oiled horns are covered with fragrant blossoms, and her neck is garlanded with her favorite edible leaves.

(Thiruvanmiyur, Chengalpattu)

The Indians' reverence for their three hundred million cattle is often misunderstood in the West. Not only are cows the symbols of Shiva, the supreme god of creation and destruction, and as such considered sacred (Hindus believe it is a sacrilege to kill them), but they are also integral to many aspects of village life. Cattle pull carts; give milk, an essential protein for vegetarians; and provide power for farming (in plowing, harvesting, grinding, and irrigation). Their manure is also used as fertilizer and is a primary fuel source. Perhaps the fact that they are treated with respect and affection and are in no danger of being eaten accounts for their seeming more intelligent than Western cattle —their eyes alert, not glazed. Here, an elderly widow who has given up her village home and family to devote the rest of her life to the worship of Shiva shares a special moment with her cow. (Varanasi District, Uttar Pradesh)

Nothing is wasted in India. Everything is used, every aspect of every object worked on, worked with, stretched to its limit, and made useful. The environment is the base, and all adapts to it. Houses in Indian villages are made entirely of indigenous materials, and thus vary according to specific climate. Where walls in the north may be built of stone or local brick, providing insulation from extremes in weather, in the south they are often made only of mats woven of local fibers and are removable so as to take advantage of prevailing winds during the hot season. Roofs in myriad shapes are made of locally fired tiles, brick, adobe, stone, wood, or a variety of thatch materials, depending upon the locale, each structured perfectly to suit the climatic region. (For example, in tornado areas roofs are lightweight, made of topical foliage, and supported separately from the low walls so that gale-force winds will take the easily replaceable roof and leave the house intact.) In this way, each aspect of the village is similarly attuned to its environs, usually achieving an ecological balance, and all the various elements collectively produce a regional style that becomes the village's trademark.

The whole concept of time in traditional India is different from that in the contemporary West. Villagers do not express a need for immediacy in product or action. The pace of life is comparatively slow, with patience an unquestioned base. Perspective in the framework of traditional Indian time is involved with the acceptance of the nature of one's surroundings: the elaborate rituals prescribed to cleanse and purify oneself before prayer and before food; the hours of preparation for every meal,

grinding and mixing spices and blending them with vegetables to simmer slowly over a dung fire; the tilling of a field with a wooden plow drawn by a bullock. Both change and permanence must be understood in direct relation to this lack of urgency. Actions are undertaken for their own merits, with concern for energy and duration subordinate to the action itself. Time seems to have a layered quality, with history, the present, and the future overlapping.

Underlying every aspect of Indian culture is an implicit faith. The ways in which this faith expresses itself are as diverse as the number of people. There is no religious norm, no basic point of view, no common belief, yet faith is inherent in everything. In the contemporary West skepticism is the norm; we are taught to analyze and, through analysis, to learn. For the most part, people in Indian villages do not question: they believe. The four qualities that seem most clearly to define faith in Indian villages are acceptance, adaptation, self-denial, and interdependence. Villagers accept their position in life and what happens to them, adapt smoothly to the demands of circumstance and crisis, are capable of almost limitless sacrifice when working towards a particular aim, and approach most aspects of their environment (societal, natural, and material) with a symbiotic care. To an extraordinary degree, villagers are content with what is present and utilize it fully (a trait not to be confused with our Western adage of "living for the present"). Indeed, one of the things I have found most surprising about India in my travels is the general happiness and good humor that prevails, even in the face of hardship, in rural areas

37

throughout the subcontinent.

The study of India is the study of religions; the two are inseparable. India is the birthplace of three major religions—Hinduism, Buddhism, and Jainism—and of many less pervasive religions, such as those of its tribal peoples. It has also provided an environment where foreign doctrines such as Islam and Christianity have been able to flourish. The core of India, and the religion of most people dealt with in this book, is Hinduism, literally translated "pertaining to Hind [India]." A precept of orthodox Hinduism is that it embraces all the religions of India, that all are simply parts of the whole. In practice, this precept has a history of deviations. The tenet is, however, fundamental to an understanding of the many facets, often conflicting, of this complex religion. Eighty-four percent of all Indians consider themselves Hindu (eleven percent are Muslim; two percent Christian; two percent tribal; and one percent other), but beyond that statement, few generalities can be made. Most descriptions of Hinduism emphasize its polytheism, and the impression that many people have is that its adherents worship thousands of gods. This is not the case, for although there are indeed thousands of deities in Hinduism's pantheon, taking into account all its many subsects, each person worships only a select few.

Orthodox Hinduism is divided into two main sects: Shaivism (comprised of the devotees of Shiva, the Creator and Destroyer) and Vaishnavism (comprised of the devotees of Vishnu, the god of preservation and continuity). Less recognized by orthodox specialists, but nevertheless prominent in worship throughout rural India, is Devi, the feminine principle sometimes referred to as the Mother Goddess or Earth Goddess. Moreover, many Hindu gods are androgynous, the absolute complement of masculine and feminine energies which join together to create life, so that gods are often worshiped with their consorts. Conveniently, most of the gods are thought of as incarnations or emanations of either Shiva, Vishnu, or Devi. In this way, for example, one of Shiva's consorts is Parvati, and among his many forms are Rudra (the Roaring One), Pashupati (Lord of the Beasts), and Nataraja (Lord of the Dance). He is worshiped as the Linga, the phallic symbol of creation and fertility, and within his "family" of lesser gods are the bull Nandi, representing fertility and strength, and Ganesha, the elephant-headed Remover of Obstacles, god of prosperity and happiness. Similarly, Vishnu's incarnations include Rama, the hero of the *Ramayana* (a primary epic of Hindu mythology), and Krishna, the dark-skinned, romantic cow-herder god, who, like Christ, is said to have lived on earth in human form; in these two forms his consorts include Sita and Radha. Vishnu also assumes the forms of animals such as Narasimha (the Invincible Lion) and Vahara (the Cosmic Boar). His associate "family" includes Hanuman, his messenger in monkey form, and Garuda, his bird-headed mount. Devi, the Mother Goddess, is also worshiped in many forms, including Lakshmi, the Lotus Goddess of home and fortune; Kali, the terrifying goddess of destruction, who brings disease and misery but also heals and blesses; Durga, the Slayer of the Buffalo Demon, a female warrior who represents indomi-

Sculptures in village shrines are often simplified versions of forms appearing in classical sculpture. Although villagers will travel to classical temples on pilgrimage and for special festivals, their daily offerings, prayers, meditations, and expectations revolve around local deities. These stone images of Sibo and Mata (the local equivalents of Shiva and his consort Parvati) have been covered in oil, vermilion, and jasmine blossoms during worship. Sibo's face is composed of cowry shells plastered onto the surface of the stone. (Puri District, Orissa)

table strength in a world of hardships; and Shakti, Creative Energy. In her innumerable incarnations, Devi is the preeminent village deity. Most Hindu families will focus only on those few deities within one of the sects to which they particularly respond either through heredity or adoption. In India Westerners are often told that the "million gods" should be regarded only as facets of the one God, or Supreme Universal Soul, referred to as Brahma or Paramahatma. This explanation is an oversimplification by most Hindus' standards, but it does convey the idea that individual gods are specific aspects or qualities of the Divine which are isolated in order to be directly approached. If this can be understood, then perhaps the whole concept of polytheism is not so formidable.

In rural India Hindu villagers are aware of orthodox gods, but often place more importance on local deities and spirits. Deities from the larger Hindu pantheon are worshiped more among the higher castes than the lower. For the village Hindu everything has a soul, an energy inherent in it, so that everything is worthy of consideration, and much is worthy of reverence. It is this attitude of consideration and reverence that imbues each man's work with a sense of purpose and gives so many of the elements of each village, both social and physical, a creative harmony. What is held sacred by a particular villager depends upon what he has learned to venerate through the influences of family, community, and the broader society. Men renowned for their wisdom and heroes of legendary battles have been compared so frequently to gods through centuries of reverential oral history that in time they are actually remembered as gods. Specific stones or trees, as well as other natural phenomena, are worshiped for their healing powers. Water held by the earth is seen as the embodiment of the Mother Goddess, so that a neighborhood spring, pond, or stream may be viewed as sacred and worshiped for its strength and fertility. Each god, goddess, or spirit is the subject of stories which clothe it in a familiar setting and thus express its direct relationship to the village. In a village in Madhya Pradesh, for example, a simple stone image of a goddess named Dharti, meaning "earth," is said to have risen from the village pond on a lotus in the distant past. Villagers are proud that she chose to reveal herself in their village and have written songs praising her beauty. She is worshiped for fertility and abundance, her attributes clearly suggesting her parallel to the goddess Lakshmi in the orthodox Hindu pantheon. In this way, each village has dozens of different places for *puja*, the act of worship—stones, trees, tiny shrines—each honored by its own followers drawn from separate castes and lineage groups. In some cases one villager may not even be aware of the existence of a god worshiped by another. In villages throughout India each god is inseparable from the traditions and legends of its origin, a source of sustenance for the unique identity of each rural area, village, caste, or family.

Three primary tenets of Hinduism are *dharma*, moral and religious duty or law, *karma*, the belief that one's actions in this life and previous lives govern the status of one's next life, and *varna*, the explicit ordering of society into classes or castes. A sense of duty underlies every action in village India. 39

What one is and what one does is precisely prescribed through tradition and ritual. (Anywhere in India, when a foreigner thanks someone for one of the frequent kindnesses showered upon him, the most common response is: "Don't thank me. It is my duty.") Duty is inextricably bound to the concept of *karma*; it is the moral duty of every Hindu to conduct a good and responsible life within the bounds of his position so that he may acquire merit with the gods and be reborn in a better position. Integral to the Hindu concept of reincarnation is the belief that one's soul evolves through each life, gaining experience through hardship, so that eventually it reaches perfection and release (called *moksha*) from rebirth and becomes one with the Supreme Universal Soul (Brahma). Much of India's resignation in the face of severe hardship is a direct result of this belief in reincarnation. Interestingly, however, a number of village surveys have shown that many uneducated Indians place more value on simple duty and its consequent merit with the gods in helping them solve their immediate problems than they do on hopes for a more fortunate rebirth.

For outsiders one of the most bewildering aspects of Indian society is caste. Caste is social order in India, the identification of each person by his hereditary qualifications, generally organized by origin and occupation. Indian society is segmented by caste into a generally hierarchical order. The classical approach is to view all Indians as belonging to one of four major categories, or *varnas:* Brahmans (priests and teachers), Kshatriyas (leaders and warriors), Vaishyas (merchants), and Shudras (farmers, craftsmen, and laborers). Within each of these four *varnas* are tens of thousands of subcategories, *jatis*, each with its own assigned position in relation to the rest. This classical overview of the social order has its limitations and is frequently disputed by scholars, but it is the simplest way to describe this complexity. The caste system is impossibly intricate, prohibiting even the Indian government from completing a comprehensive classification. Its very existence is a paramount example of the Indians' love of detail. Indian marriage is usually endogamous, which in rural areas means that a person must marry within his caste, but usually outside his village. The strictures of caste, therefore, encourage an interregional unity within the subcontinent, for there is a constant flow of members from one village to the next in any given area. The multiplicity of castes is the result of an ancient history and the repeated overlapping of cultures. The original peoples of each district had their own social order. Added to these were the social institutions introduced by the repeated migrations of people from other areas; each migration in turn became defined by its own origins and by its subsequent new position within the society.

Inextricably bound to the notion of caste are the concepts of purity and pollution. Hinduism regulates one's life into a prescribed pattern of what is right and wrong. Each person must live as pure a life as possible, and there are many prohibitions for each caste, especially among the highest castes. (A sketchy parallel might be made to the Jewish system regarding kosher food and the prohibition against pork.) To transgress these prohibitions is to become polluted, and the cleansing of this state requires rigorous ritual. The relative status of a given caste is ordered through custom, such as the way in which food or water is served and consumed, language phrased, or dress, jewelry, and hair worn. Caste survives through mutual recognition and interdependence.

Outside the traditional caste system are still further categories that include tribal peoples, Christians, Muslims (although Christians and Muslims have evolved a parallel "caste" system of their own), and Untouchables. Perhaps the most infamous aspect of Indian society is Untouchability. Historically, the Untouchables' position in society was so low (they swept houses and streets, removed garbage, cleaned the sewers, and did other "polluting" jobs) that they were prohibited from ever coming into physical contact with a person of higher caste. Since independence, however, the Indian constitution has abolished Untouchability, renaming members of this caste Harijans, or "God's people," and giving them many more social and cultural opportunities. The government has outlawed discrimination against caste in public places, and in a program somewhat akin to affirmative action in the United States, vacancies in colleges and public service posts are reserved for Harijans. Low-caste and Harijan peoples now have an equal say in Indian government and their situation is slowly improving. Prejudice is still common in rural India between castes (for example, villagers may refuse to accept work which is prohibited by their caste and those of separate castes may refuse to drink from the same well), but many caste distinctions have broken down, and lower-caste peoples have many more

freedoms. Tribal peoples stand outside this caste system, the term caste really referring to social position within a wide-reaching and complex society. Most tribes, in contrast, are comprised of geographically limited groups of people and have social and cultural systems that, in most cases, antedate classical Hinduism.

It should also be pointed out that, although India's social system is perhaps more formalized than most, it is not without parallel in other societies, even until fairly recently within Europe. Movement within the social structure has been and still can be achieved, although it is subject to the same slow time frame as everything else in India. Caste definition in rural India is based upon a precise position within a small framework. A villager who travels from his home takes with him his caste and village identity. This gives him a point of reference in the strange new society in which he finds himself. Yet as he lives and works at a distant place, an experience common to many villagers, hereditary social barriers often become less rigid and he may be able to fraternize with castes that it would have been inconceivable for him to associate with at home. In rural communities a definite hierarchy still exists among Brahmans, landowners, merchants, farmers and craftsmen, and laborers, but each is so dependent on the other that, although friction sometimes occurs, society runs smoothly as a whole.

As mentioned earlier, the traditional priests of orthodox Hinduism are Brahmans, a social class, or caste, formed in about 1000 B.C. It is the duty of Brahmans to preserve the purity of traditional Hinduism. Although their elaborate rituals are minutely prescribed in ancient Sanskrit texts, their prayers, songs, and rites are recited from memory. By ensuring their own absolute purity in all matters (purity being more important even than spirituality) Brahman priests maintain the continuity of the Hindu social order. (Although Brahmans are traditionally associated with the priesthood and teaching, the majority today are employed in occupations, such as land management, that are unrelated to religion. All Brahmans, however, regardless of their profession, have a high-caste status and occupy privileged positions within the society.) While some of the shrines in a village, often the wealthier ones, are presided over by local Brahmans, others are administered by lower-caste, non-Brahman priests. These priests are drawn to their vocations in a number of ways. Some inherit the care and devotion of their deity through family, while others gain piety through visions or prophecies. Although Brahman priests are always male, non-Brahman priests can be, and in some villages are, women (though, generally, women function as priestesses only for the less orthodox deities). Barbers often double as the traditional priests of lower-caste shrines and are sought after to perform rituals, healings, and prophecies on behalf of the gods or goddesses of their particular shrines. In all cases the primary function of a priest involves the care and adoration of his deity. In important shrines the priest performs *puja* (the act of worship) to the icon twice daily, morning and evening. His preparations for *puja* include washing the image, dressing it, adorning it with flowers, and offering it suitable sacred foods (coconuts, bananas, milk, or other items, which have been brought in offering); this is usually accompanied by prescribed movements with a lighted lamp and incense. In the shrines of less important deities, or gods associated with a particular season or disease, *puja* may be performed only weekly or even yearly. Devotees line up to pass before the icon, at which time they give food or flowers to be blessed; the newly blessed food (*prasad*) is then eaten by the devotees (some is left for the priest as a tithe) and the nonedible offerings are taken home, where they act as a blessing on the household. In shrines dedicated to Shiva, or any of his incarnations, devotees are given sacred ash from the ceremony which they then smear on their foreheads in reverence.

Rituals introduce important moments of every village day. From the reciting of early morning prayers to household deities and the drawing of rice-powder designs on the dirt in front of the house before anyone leaves to the blessing of tools or the offering of fruit to the god of crop fertility, the beginning of each task is sanctified by ritual. Seasons are dramatic in India, each completely altering the environment. A village, seen caked and dry in the hot season, its walls seeming to blend into the dust of the road, is transformed during the constant monsoon rains into rich tones of brown and green. The environment is such an integral part of village life that culture has evolved around variations in nature. As seasons change, each is recognized by a special ceremony dedicated to its essence; for example, the tilling of the fields, the planting of new crops, the coming of rains, and the nurturing, harvesting, winnowing, and storing of produce are all

Monsoon rains hit most of India in June, July, August, and
September. Areas of heavy rainfall, such as Orissa, have as much
rain in four months as Oregon has in five years. In coastal
Orissa villages and roads are built as often as possible on raised
ground to prevent their being flooded. These men are sheltered
under traditional Orissan umbrellas made of palm leaves.

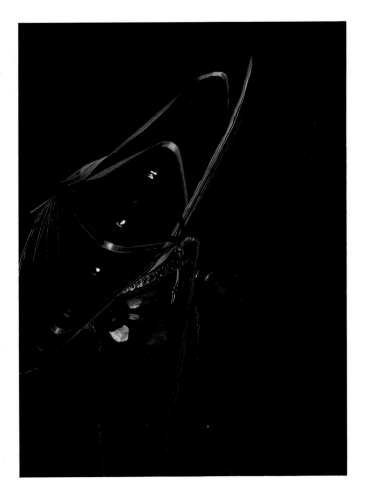

Left: In Karnataka a *yakshagana* actor, who will play the role of a legendary princess, spends hours laboriously putting on his costume and makeup before each performance. At this stage, after two hours, he has only half-finished dressing. His troupe is an itinerant one, traveling from village to village and portraying in dramatic form the myths and histories of local heritage.

Below, left: The essence of Indian tribal culture lies in its poetry and music. Although most tribal peoples are illiterate, every aspect of their daily lives is recorded in poetry and set to song. In the Jhodia tribe's village of Renga in Koraput District, Orissa, two girls play one-stringed gourd instruments, accompanied by two drums and a brass horn, and sing, "My heart is like a ripe red flower. Pluck me."

Below, right: As a part of a ritual vow (*vrata*) to Bommula, a local god in Ganjam District, Orissa, women have tied unfired, painted figures of villagers and farm animals to a tree to ensure crop fertility and general good health.

attended by ritual. Festivals are frequent in India: joyous, crowded, and colorful celebrations with villagers joining together to honor the gods or the seasons. Each stage in every villager's life (birth, puberty, betrothal, marriage, illness, tragedy, and death) is also marked by a prescribed ritual. With these ceremonies of transition, through the repetitions of words, songs, gestures, and actions, archaic customs become fused with the contemporary, providing a common bond between villagers and their heritage.

Villages are often most alive at night. Many communities and households are still without modern media, although this situation is rapidly changing. In the virtual absence of books, radios, television, or films, people delight in their ancient resources: stories, poetry, drama, and dance. Handed down from generation to generation, recounted myths and legends give expression to people's passions, hopes, and dreams as well as justifying their traditions and beliefs. The memory of the illiterate mind is incredible. Children are taught from infancy to repeat stories, poems, and songs verbatim, so that by the time they reach maturity many have memorized whole epics the size of the Bible. Evenings and the many festivals and holy days are filled with the recitation of these legends and songs describing the deeds of gods and heroes. Dramas and dances retelling ancient tales, often composed centuries, even millennia, ago, are reenacted by traveling troupes on the edges of villages. Villagers will watch enthralled all night, for as long as twelve hours at a time, excitedly yelling responses to the actors' lines from these well-known stories.

Singing is an important part of many daytime activities as well, breaking the monotony of hard work. Each activity, among them planting, plowing, driving carts, and rowing boats, has its own song, handed down for countless generations. Women have special songs for their children, concerning their housework, and about their separation from parents or husbands. Love songs, often beautiful and sad, are sung by both sexes, and whole families or communities join together to sing prayers to ward off disease or disaster or on days devoted to special gods. Many villagers, particularly women, perform fasts and engage in periods of prayer in accordance with ritual vows, or *vrata*, in which they appeal to a god with hopes of gaining a specific favor (a cure for themselves or their children, or perhaps a job for an unemployed husband). *Vrata* rituals are filled with songs praising the honored gods and are accompanied by other prescribed customs, such as the decorating of houses with devotional designs or the donating of sacrificial terracotta elephants to the river.

An example of oral tradition can be found in the three-day festival of Raja Parab in Orissa beginning on the last day of Jyaishtha (May to June). Orissans believe that Devi, the Earth Goddess, starts her three-day menstrual cycle on the first day of Raja Parab. During this cycle the earth is considered unclean, as are menstruating Indian women, and is not supposed to be touched. While the festival lasts, there is a prohibition against going barefoot, plowing, digging, or even using clay pots, and all work is suspended. The three days are spent in the

A young Rajput bridegroom is transported by festooned camel to his wedding at the bride's village in Jaisalmer District, Rajasthan. The long rifle carried by his father and brother on the accompanying camel is symbolic of Rajput military prowess.

performing of time-honored stories, songs, and dances dedicated to the goddess and are attended by feasts and sports. Raja Parab is also called the Swing Festival, for swings are placed in the trees for children and young couples, the latter singing duets. The festival ends with a ceremonial plowing of new fields to honor the renewed fertility of the Earth Goddess.

It is difficult for most Indian villagers to divide their self-images from their environment, to view the material world as separate from the emotional. The world is not divided, as it is in the West, into man, who has reason and a soul, and objects, which do not. In rural India all aspects of the environment are considered parts of the whole and everything has a value, a personal meaning, the portent of which either helps or hinders an individual's life. Astrology, palmistry, and frequent consultations of the gods through their priests are essential to most activities in rural India. In fact, the whole cycle of life in an Indian village is governed by what in the West might be termed superstition. In order to live safely and not to anger the gods, demons, or malevolent ancestor-spirits, every action is prescribed (for example, the manner in which to enter a house, how to cross one's legs, or the way in which to look at another person's small children so as not to be accused of having the evil eye). A farmer must consult his horoscope, *janma patrika,* in order to decide the best time to plant his crop, to harvest it, or even to build his house. Apart from the countless minor omens or changes that often require someone to consult a seer of some kind, there are twenty-one essential ceremonies in life for which it

is necessary to have astrological charts prepared. Of the many ceremonies that require auspicious signs to be charted the most important are those involving marriage.

Virtually all marriages in Indian villages are arranged by the parents of the couple to be wed. The horoscopes of the boy and girl under consideration are researched and compared to assure both families that the couple is well matched and that the two will lead successful lives together. The most important considerations are longevity, work and income, and children. Weddings are usually very expensive for a bride's family, the cost directly related to the family's caste status and income. The bride must be given new clothes and jewelry, and the groom and his family must be given a dowry, often very sizable. Among poorer families the groom might receive a radio, watch, and bicycle, while cash must be given to his father. Wealthier families would expect cattle, bullock carts, or even a motorcycle or car. After the betrothal has been arranged the marriage festivities involve the whole village, each local craftsman and tradesman performing a different task. On the day of the wedding the groom is sumptuously dressed and, surrounded by family and friends, may either ride a horse or be carried in a palanquin to the house of the bride. The house is often repainted for the occasion and is adorned with leaves and flowers. The bride, in most areas of India, is dressed in red and veiled, and the couple is married while being led around a sacred fire by priests chanting Sanskrit verses. The newlyweds garland each other with flowers to signify their union; the bride is then given glass bangles to wear

47

Opposite: A young married woman in Udaipur District wears a machine-printed *sari* and a large gold nose ring. Her openness is symptomatic of the changing attitudes towards women in Rajasthan (a state where women have traditionally been secluded), especially in areas of increased tourism

Right: Children begin at an early age to help around the house, care for their younger siblings, and tend the animals. Here, a young girl carries back the water she has been sent to fetch from a village tank in Karnataka.

on her wrists, and vermilion powder is placed on her forehead and in the part of her hair. After a noisy and excited evening, sometimes accompanied by fireworks, the bride leaves with the groom to return to his family's house, technically never to return to that of her own parents.

Women in Indian villages are secondary citizens. Hinduism teaches a woman to treat her husband as a god. It is her duty to obey him and care for him and his family. A new bride in a household is considered inferior to her husband's mother, aunts, and sisters, and advantage is often taken of her. She is under the strict supervision of her mother-in-law, who makes sure that she treats her new husband well and learns the regimen of household chores. As she grows older, however, and has gained the family's respect, she can emerge as a very powerful figure both within the family and, in a subtle way, within the community. It is considered essential that a wife produce a male child because funeral rites in Hinduism—critical to the successful passage of the soul from one life to the next—are only considered entirely efficacious when performed by the eldest male child in the immediate family of the deceased. A woman who cannot have children is thought to be inauspicious, and in some areas people will not associate with her. (Barrenness can even be grounds for annulment.) The same is true of a young widow, who is regarded as having caused her husband's misfortune. While many of the villages of northern India that are under strong Muslim influence have adopted the practice of *purdah*—requiring that women wear veils and be kept out of sight of nonfamily males—this custom is not

indigenous to India and, where practiced, has been losing favor in this century. Although women in rural India might well be considered oppressed by contemporary Western standards, they are relatively free in comparison to their Middle Eastern counterparts. A woman's role is subordinate, but she regards herself with dignity and is greatly honored in Hindu society. Her duties, in addition to childbearing, include preparing meals, cleaning and maintaining the house, caring for her children, helping with her husband's tasks (such as planting or harvesting rice, or spinning cotton for the loom), perhaps washing and mending clothes (depending on her caste), buying food and provisions, and participating in the rituals of the home and village, many of which are solely the prerogative of women.

Children are given responsibilities at an early age in India. They are integral to the survival of the family and are treated as equal members. Although more and more children are going to school, they are still required to aid in the running of the household, to care for the family's animals, and to help with the work. Babies are adored, but not coddled; children loved, but not condescended to. Minor accidents are treated with humor instead of alarm, and children learn to regard misfortune with tolerance. Children in India, as in the West, are taught values and customs through stories and songs. A major difference, however, is apparent in the way in which these stories are conceived. In the West, stories—whether they involve adventures to another land or are simply about the lives of other people—are usually presented as self-contained units, as something outside the child with which he

Above: Young goatherder boys in coastal Orissa regularly spend the whole day far from the village herding and grazing their families' goats on dune grasses by the sea, returning home only after dark. Unlike southern Indians, Orissans are usually not vegetarians. They eat fish and mutton, but not chicken.

Left: Two old men at a seasonal cattle and buffalo market in Gaya District, Bihar, discuss the merits of different bullocks. Most rural houses do not have chairs. Instead, villagers all over India squat, a position they are able to maintain comfortably for hours.

Opposite: Hindus are ritually cremated at death. Strict religious custom requires that the eldest son of the bereaved family officiate at the funeral, because only his performance of the funeral rites is thought to ensure the successful release of the soul from earthly bondage. The man shown here is tending the funeral pyre of his father.

can nonetheless identify and learn. In village India, however, stories teach a child that he is related to everything else. In them the sun is said to be his brother, the moon his sister, the trees his brothers, all animals his cousins, and so on. With the world explained to him in this way and through his participation at an early age in the frequent religious rituals of his household, the beliefs, customs, and traditions of Hinduism are transmitted, becoming pivotal to his outlook on life.

Old age is respected in India. In villages most people still live in extended families with everyone related to the male line (uncles, aunts, and cousins) under the same roof. Hindus care for the aged in their families, looking to them for advice and for help in caring for the small children. Of all Hindu rites, those concerning death are the most complex and carefully followed. Sacred texts say that if a Hindu dies in the holy city of Varanasi (also known as Benares) and his ashes are scattered in the Ganges River, his soul will be released from rebirth and reach ultimate bliss. Aged people from all over India make a last pilgrimage to that city in order to die there. It is important first that a dying person be moved from his bed to the ground, so that he may be in contact with the spirit of the earth. Upon death, his corpse is then wrapped in cotton and carried by male relatives to the cremation ground at the edge of the village, and put if possible beside a river or stream. Before being placed on a pyre of wood (often a very expensive item in arid parts of the subcontinent) the body is either immersed in or sprinkled with water. The eldest son (or, in his absence, the deceased person's closest male relative in the next

generation) initiates all the rituals. He circles the pyre, makes some offerings to the spirit of the dead relative, and lights the fire. His principal duty, which only he can perform, is to burst the flaming corpse's skull with a rod to ensure the release of the soul. After the flames have subsided, he scatters the ashes in a river, if necessary traveling far to reach one. The family of the deceased is considered impure for many days after the funeral, during which time they must cease their normal activities. On a given day, which varies in custom, a purification rite is performed and ancestors are honored with prayers asking them to welcome the new soul to their number.

Indian rural culture permits a surprising amount of movement and transition in society. Small villages which seem, at first glance, to have populations which have remained isolated and unchanged for many centuries are in reality undergoing constant shifts and renewals. These changes occur for two main reasons. First, as expressed earlier, men in rural areas usually marry women from villages other than their own. In most cases they are not closely related, but they are both either from the same caste or from a caste with a similar social/ occupational standing, and the bride comes to live with the man's family in his village. Second, it is common today, as it has been throughout Indian history, for a tradesman, craftsman, servant, or laborer to keep his family in his hereditary village but to spend as much as eleven-and-a-half months each year, or even successive years, at a distant place of employment without returning home. Many of the great monuments and lasting works of art from

Left: A weaver in Aurangabad District, Maharashtra, winds thread onto a spindle before setting up his loom to weave brocaded cotton *himru* shawls. These shawls are a local cottage industry and have become increasingly popular among Indian women.

Opposite: The wife of a Kumbhar (member of the local potter's caste) from Kutch, Gujarat, uses a long stick dipped in white lime to apply a second layer of design to a previously fired pot.

earlier epochs in sites all over India were created and/or worked on by itinerant villagers. Most of the fresh ideas leading to innovations and adaptations in rural style and custom have been transmitted through these two primary forms of contact with the broader world.

Indian villages display an extraordinary diversity and abundance of creativity. Meager incomes and the limitations imposed by available materials are offset by an elaborate richness in custom and ritual. In other societies the orthodox Islamic restrictions against figural representation in art fostered the development of advanced concepts in geometric art. Similarly, in Indian villages restrictions caused by isolation, environment, customs, ideals, and economy have generated a profusion of artistic forms and decoration that are applied to almost every aspect of village life. Traditionally, each village, or close group of villages, had living within it all the craftsmen necessary to provide it with everything it required. Although in contemporary India many of those craftsmen have been forced to change their occupations because of the competition arising from mass-production, many of the traditional crafts are still being practiced. In villages crafts have always been learned within the hereditary family. Formerly, the sons and grandsons of a craftsman such as a weaver had no choice but to become weavers. In contemporary India, with economic and cultural demands forcing some craftsmen to look for employment outside the family's customary line of work, the witnessing and learning of many crafts by the young is dwindling.

In India artistry is not egocentric. The highest

ideal for a craftsman or artist is to re-create or reproduce perfectly a traditional form, with the extent of labor immaterial in comparsion to the achievement of a fine result. Many rural crafts have a religious aspect and, in theory, only perfect images, without blemish, can be offered to the gods. In practice the items produced are frequently, though unintentionally, imbued with the style of their creator. Art and craft work is never signed; it would never occur to the artist to do so. Rural forms are often free of the nonessential, melding an economy of line with a spontaneity not found in Indian classical art. Many of the village crafts shown in the following photographs portray this unselfconscious sense of form and personal abstraction.

Both craftsmen and householders find ways to decorate and enhance objects of daily and seasonal use. No detail is overlooked. Even walls of simple mud and dung are often decorated in intricate patterns of rice powder, which the women of the village apply with their fingers. Created as part of seasonal devotions, these decorations are temporary, often wearing away from one season to the next. Local carpenters carve designs on beams, brackets, and doors as well as on equipment such as carts, plows, and wooden mortars. The potter's art is refined in Indian villages, where low-fire vessels are produced in myriad shapes, often graceful and paper thin. The brass and copper pots used by women everywhere to carry and contain water vary in shape and decoration in each district. (Plastic buckets, now popular in villages because they are so much lighter for carrying water, are being made today in

traditional pot shapes.) On simple wooden looms village weavers produce colorful cotton *saris* worn by women and plain cloth for men, as well as the exquisite silks used for weddings and special festivals. The remnants of worn-out clothes are bleached, pieced together, and profusely embroidered by village mothers and their daughters to serve as part of the latters' dowries. And these are only a few examples of village craftsmanship and creativity.

Although education is a major priority of both the central and state governments, and massive funding has been directed towards the opening of new schools and the expansion of existing ones, illiteracy is still widespread in villages throughout India. Only twenty-nine percent of the entire population is literate. (This statistic varies, however, from state to state: in Kerala, for example, there is a sixty percent literacy rate, while in Rajasthan, the figure is only twenty-four percent.) Population growth combined with the inaccessiblity of some areas and the intransigence of others have inhibited the rapid spread of education. Nevertheless, progress is being made. The literacy rate in some areas is climbing as much as one percent per year, and at present the increase in literacy is outstripping the rise in population.

As might be expected, one of the most pressing problems in India today is overpopulation. Approximately 750 million people, nearly three times the number living in the United States, reside in a country only one third its size. India's population has doubled in the thirty-eight years since independence and tripled in the last century alone. The effect this has had upon the rural economy, society, and culture cannot be overemphasized. Everything has suffered because of it. It is all the more remarkable, then, that despite this appalling growth rate India now has a food surplus. For the first time in this century its villages, although poor, are no longer destitute. Historically India was a wealthy country, its rural cultures self-sufficient and thriving. Overpopulation and mass impoverishment have resulted as much, if not more, from external influences as from indigenous conditions. Today central government and international birth control campaigns have been introduced in almost every Indian village, and attitudes are slowly changing, but these campaigns are fighting an uphill battle against entrenched religious and social customs. The sheer magnitude of the population and its frightening growth rate defy easy solution and as yet the inroads made by birth control have not proved sufficient to reverse this upward trend.

Crowded conditions, imbalanced diets, and the semitropical climate of India, with its extreme heat and humidity, have created a virtual breeding ground for virus and bacteria. Disease poses a constant threat to villagers, but remedies from various sources are available. *Ayurvedic* medicine, an ancient science whose roots can be traced to the earliest Indian epics, the *Vedas*, is in widespread use throughout the subcontinent and has a number of effective treatments. Local cures distilled from herbs and minerals are also popular. Religion still provides the majority of villagers with a core of belief, and most regional sects and rural customs are filled with promises of cures for illness and misfortune if proper reverence is shown and the necessary rituals

Opposite, above: Almost every village in southern India has a temple to the goddess of epidemics, known as Mariammai in Andhra Pradesh. She is a cruel goddess (often associated with Durga, the goddess of destruction) and is given offerings to propitiate her. Most villages devote a special day every year to her worship. A young priest dressed as Mariammai runs through a coastal market chasing the demon of cholera and soliciting worshipers to give offerings to his shrine. (Chittivalasa, Vishakhapatnam District, Andhra Pradesh)

Opposite, below: Open markets are the source for most commodities in rural India. While remote villages pool their resources, conducting their own weekly markets, people in communities near a town travel to the daily markets there to buy necessities. Vegetables and fruits are brought to the town markets from surrounding farms. Farmers generally sell their produce to a vendor and spend the day enjoying the market rather than hawking the goods themselves. (Mysore District, Karnataka)

Above: Arica nuts, on display in small bins in this vendor's stall in Mysore District, Karnataka, are usually mixed with a sweet or spicy paste and wrapped in green betul leaves. Chewed by villagers throughout the subcontinent, they are a slight narcotic, like tobacco.

Right: Powdered dyes are used for cosmetic purposes (to make the beauty mark on a woman's forehead or to supply the red added to the part of her hair signifying marriage) and for dyeing cloth. Incense, sold in stick form, is considered an important purifying agent and is used during daily prayers. (Mysore District, Karnataka)

only rarely and are owned by government officials and wealthy landlords. Most villagers travel on foot, by bullock cart, or by the increasingly popular bicycle, unless they are going far, in which case they use the trains or buses. In almost all areas traditional farming methods predominate. In some states, particularly in the northwest, farmers with government aid have joined together in order to be able to afford tractors and other machinery, which they then share among themselves to farm their lands. Agrarian modernization in most villages, however, means a metal blade for a plow, metal axles for a cart, or improved-yield crop strains for planting. Synthetic machine-made cloth is increasingly popular throughout India, and plastics are now so pervasive that the traditional crafts of pottery and metalwork are in danger of becoming obsolete.

More and more, modern attitudes are reaching remote villages. Improved transportation and communications are partly responsible, but perhaps more than anything else, it is through film and radio that new cultural values are disseminated. Most villagers have access to the cinema, shown in their meeting halls, in tents set up on village outskirts, or in theaters in neighboring towns. Bombay churns out at least one Hindi movie every day, while regional cities produce popular films in local languages. Most movies made in India are musicals and, like those made in America during the Depression, portray idealized affluent societies. The music from these films is beginning to be heard in traditional villages, on radios and cassette recorders (which have become more widely available in the last two decades). It is too early to know the full impact that this increased media exposure will have on rural Indian traditions. Certainly it has caused villagers to question their heritage and customs. Increasingly, traditional songs and dances are being supplanted by new ones, the demand for age-old crafts and designs is being replaced with the desire for Westernized elitist styles, and cities are becoming even more crowded as a result of an influx of villagers trying to find the luxuries depicted in the movies. On the positive side, films and radio help to offset the country's massive illiteracy, making villagers aware of other aspects of India and of the world and more conscious of national and international affairs.

For whatever reason, each year more hereditary customs are superceded by new ones. Regional characteristics are discarded in favor of widespread popular styles. Western-style pants and shirts are replacing *dhotis, lungis,* and *kurtas.* Silver jewelry, which ten years ago identified a woman by her village and caste, is seldom seen. Buildings of brick, poured cement, and tile multiply in villages previously made of local mud and thatch. With these changes come new attitudes and approaches. The scope of each village is broader, its boundaries opened, and its regimentation and factionalism challenged. Growing awareness tends to encourage tolerance. Yet in order for true progress to be made modernization must be tempered with an understanding of rural heritage and a blending of those fine qualities and techniques that have been developed during thousands of years of indigenous civilization. A modern steel blade for a wooden plow still pulled by a bullock and improved grains and irrigating techniques may be more valuable than an expensive tractor. Traditional houses built of mud with separately supported thatched roofs are more practical to an earthquake- and hurricane-prone environment than the popular and costly new concrete structures which crack and fall in severe storms and are difficult to replace.

India's five hundred thousand villages portray an overwhelming diversity of form, style, custom, and ritual. Each is a product of a long evolution, an overlapping of separate peoples and cultures over a period of thousands of years. Contemporary rural India is a mirror of its past. Its future is dependent on a successful melding of ancient strengths with insightful innovations.

A large ceremonial arch marks the boundary of the tribal
Dongaria Kondh village of Kurli in Koraput District, Orissa, and
was erected to honor Dharmu, the principal male deity of this
tribe. Although it stands in a remote village totally cut off from
Indian culture at large, this arch is archetypal for India and the
Far East and is very similar to early Buddhist gateways of the
first century B.C.

THE EVOLUTION OF INDIAN VILLAGES

India is too often glibly referred to as a "third world" country, thus wrongly equating the external symptoms of disease, poverty, and requests for foreign aid with what in the West is considered a lack of social and cultural development. The term "third world," although generally used to refer to economy, also implies a people's inexperience and immaturity when compared with the well-established powers. India, however, has been recognized throughout history as a leader in science, industry, philosophy, and the arts. Only within the last three hundred years, under foreign imperial power, has its wealth been decimated and its cultural growth undermined. During this period, too, its population has risen beyond control and poverty has become pervasive. Since the attainment of independence in 1947, however, India has regained, against extraordinary odds, many of its cultural strengths. In a rapidly modernizing world, the Indian village has retained much of its dignity as the bastion of tradition. Although often geographically isolated, it remains the mirror of Indian culture, reflecting both a constant sense of the timeless and an ongoing adaptation to the new.

There is a widespread inherent sense of the past in India, although interest in historical research and statistics is relatively new there, introduced through Western scholarship. In order to understand fully the intricacies involved in contemporary Indian civilization, one must recognize the constant interplay of history and the present. Each separate group of villages reflects an individual history, its uniqueness often the result of cultural innovations begun centuries, if not millennia, ago. "Tradition develops like a spiral that uncoils and recoils," according to Pupul Jayakar, a leading Indian scholar, "negating the linear movement of history. Within this movement, nothing is rejected. There is transformation but never, it seems, complete destruction. There is refusal to discard or polarise issues, to confront and destroy the alien and the heretical....The atomic age exists alongside the Chalcolithic. To trace that survival, the life patterns of another age, and to witness their transformation and operation within village societies today, is to grasp the true significance of the Indian scene."

The following, then, is an outline of Indian history, focusing on the genesis of rural Indian villages: their diverse cultures, their present conditions, and the invaluable contributions they have made for the past twenty-five hundred years to the growth of Western civilization.

Man has inhabited India continuously for more than three hundred thousand years. As his evolution does not closely parallel that of early man in other areas of the world, Indian archaeologists have divided the Indian prehistoric periods slightly differently—into the Early, Middle, and Late Stone Ages. Of the two earliest ages, which lasted as late as 8000 B.C., there exist few remains, for the most part only stone tools: hand axes, pebble and flake tools, and later microliths. Descriptions of the culture of these periods are therefore mostly a matter of conjecture. Some of the first indications of a higher sophistication in early man's development can be found in cave paintings in central India, dating from 8000 to 5000 B.C. Man at this time had seemingly learned neither to cultivate nor to raise livestock,

Rice is germinated and then planted stalk by stalk in flooded paddies during the monsoon season, in the same way that it has been for thousands of years. (Bankut, Varanasi District, Uttar Pradesh)

The way in which these rammed earth houses have been built and laid out in the desert village of Som, Jaisalmer District, Rajasthan, is reminiscent of early Indus Valley communities thousands of years old. The dome-shaped building on the edge of this leather curer's courtyard is a kitchen constructed with a hole at the top to provide ventilation.

but survived solely through hunting and food-gathering. His mode of life would have been migratory; his dwellings, unsettled. The first signs of a more developed, settled society were in the northwest. The Indus Valley Civilization, as this society is called, flourished from approximately 2500 B.C. to 1500 B.C. The two major "cities" of the culture—Mohenjo Daro and Harappa—were in an area within present-day Pakistan, but by 2000 B.C. satellite settlements, some of them quite large, were sprinkled throughout northwestern India (Kalibangan in Rajasthan and Lothal in Gujarat among them). Information about this period, based mainly on excavations from major sites, suggests that there was a widespread sedentary agricultural society in these areas. During the next five hundred years, established village culture spread to cover large parts of India. Villagers learned to cultivate rice, of fundamental importance to all subsequent Indian economies, and, in the south, began to use terraced fields. Other crops were sugarcane, coconuts, bananas in all their numerous varieties, pepper, ginger, yams, millets, and several types of peas. Animals, such as cattle, oxen, buffalo, and goats, were bred and used for farming as well as for food. Techniques for pottery-making and sculpting in clay were refined, as was craftsmanship in stonecarving and bronze casting. The structure of houses varied from area to area, with fired brick and rammed earth often used for foundation walls, and wood, bamboo, and thatch for partitions and roofs. Houses in many of the present-day villages near these ancient sites are remarkably similar, as is much of the local pottery and terracotta sculpture.

By 1450 B.C. in the Deccan—India's southern plateau—cotton and flax were being spun and used for clothing (cotton would prove to be of incalculable value to the development of Indian culture).

Nomadic hordes from western Asia arrived in India at about this time. The strength and cohesion of the Indus Valley culture was waning—perhaps because of the dilution through dissemination that was taking place throughout the subcontinent and perhaps because of a series of natural disasters—and those foreign barbarians infiltrated easily. The latter, known as Aryans, were members of the huge Indo-Aryan language group from which Latin, the European languages, and Sanskrit derive. Compared to the Indians they encountered, who were living in rural communities, the Aryans were uncivilized and unsophisticated. They still lived almost exclusively by hunting and as yet had not learned many of the crafts necessary for living in a fixed village. The Aryan impact on Indian civilization, however, was enormous. Their social order—comprised of the Brahman, Kshatriya, Vaishya, and Shudra classes—gave its form to the caste system. The Aryan religion, collected in verse in the *Rig Veda*, provided the basis for orthodox Hinduism. And the legends and mythology of these people from western Asia gave to Hinduism many of its primary gods and heroes. In return, the indigenous peoples of India, through intermarriage with the Aryans, taught them the benefits of cultivation and rural settlement. This period saw one of the first great assimilations in India, a cross-fertilization of two distinct cultures.

By the year 1000 B.C. Indians were aware of the many uses of iron technology. With the resulting

63

An iron forge in a village in Bijapur District, Karnataka, has large wooden bellows carved to resemble a lion's head. Employing methods practiced centuries ago, the low-caste smith who works here makes knives, tools, and farming implements in his small furnace, pounding the molten iron into shape on the cubed anvil at the right.

new tools, geographical boundaries were expanded and wider areas of the subcontinent opened for agrarian use. Development during the next two thousand years was essentially an internal affair, revolving around the three basic groups of people then inhabiting India. The first, many non-Hindu tribal peoples, heirs to the customs and rituals of pre-Indus Valley Stone Age Indians, lived in the vast inaccessible forest regions at the peripheries of the cultivated lands. (Many of these tribes continue to maintain their cultural unity today, as will be discussed in detail in the chapter concerning the east.) The second, groups of people from pre-Aryan settled societies resistant to the new foreign influences, created isolated environments in central and south India. The third, spreading throughout the rest of the land, were the orthodox Hindu descendents of the union between nomadic Aryans and members of the preceding farming communities.

The eighth century B.C. marks the beginning of refined Hindu culture in the north. The great epics, the *Mahabharata* and the *Ramayana*, which set the standards of Hindu ethics and ideals, were already in established oral forms and were well known throughout India. The later *Vedas* and the earliest *Brahmanas*, which, among other things, specified laws to govern both state and religious ritual, were being composed and collated at this time. Feudal states with Brahman and Kshatriya aristocracy were established in the Gangetic Plain and in the west. Governed from large towns which served as centers for industry and trade, these states also encompassed smaller towns and villages radiating out from the town centers. Each village specialized in a craft such as pottery, weaving, carpentry, or weaponry and acted as a magnet for other artisans working in the same trade. These were the beginnings of artisan guilds in India, with craftsmen holding respected positions in society, as prescribed in the *Vedas*. By the seventh century B.C., trade routes covered most of northern India, joining a network of villages and towns for supply purposes. The first contact with the West was made at this time through the Achaemenid Empire in Persia, which was interested in obtaining Indian jewels, cotton, and spices. This age was one of mental and cultural expansion, the first experience of materialism and affluence for the northern Indians. Out of this new, rich society emerged two different ideologies—each philosophically opposed to extravagance, hierarchical ritual, and violence—one propounded by Guatama Buddha and the other by Mahavira. Both philosophers stood against caste and advocated a return to a simpler, more direct lifestyle —an ascetic approach focused on belief in the "One Soul"; namely, the belief that the material world, people, animals, invention, and so on are all equal parts of the great soul. The Buddhists and the Jains (as the followers of Mahavira are known) developed into massive religious cults, distinct from each other and very powerful, both altering the shape of Indian history. (Today, inhabitants of those villages in Bihar and eastern Uttar Pradesh where Buddha traveled and preached relate anecdotes of his journeys as if he had visited their villages decades, as opposed to centuries, ago.)

Persian interest in India continued well into the sixth century B.C., with Darius I extending his

A scene carved on a stone gateway to a Buddhist reliquary mound, or stupa, in Sanchi, Madhya Pradesh, depicts houses, stables, horses, and people of the first century B.C.

empire as far as the Indus Valley. Persia, still under Achaemenid rule, had traded Indian goods with Greece and kindled that country's interest. As early as 513 B.C., Skylax, the first of many Greek travelers, wrote of India's wealth. By 326 B.C., its fame had lured Alexander the Great into an attempt to extend his empire to encompass India. Although the might of massed Indian armies proved too much for him and he retreated (he died as a result of an illness contracted in what is now Pakistan), Greek lords were nevertheless left to govern small states in the far northwest, thus establishing a bridge for the trade of crafts from Indian villages to Europe. Not only did Greek styles influence India at this time, but it appears that the craft of stonecarving, later so popular in both classical and rural India, was introduced to the subcontinent by Greek craftsmen.

During this period, India was in its Golden Age. The Mauryan Empire, an indigenous Indian dynasty which subsequently grew to encompass half of the subcontinent, was founded on the Gangetic Plain and eventually established Buddhism as the official religion. It was the first empire in India to join under a single administration such broad and diverse elements. Buddhism encouraged a period of learning. Scripts were developed (Sanskrit, Prakrit, and many local variations) and literature was stressed, with both Buddhist and early Hindu texts written down for the first time. It was from the Mauryan Empire that monks traveled into eastern Asia, spreading Buddhism into Tibet, China, and Southeast Asia. Art became highly refined and numerous Mauryan sculptural masterpieces in stone and clay remain today. In his accounts the great grammarian and chronicler Panini, in the fourth century B.C., differentiated between the court artists, *raj shilpins*, and village craftsmen, *gram shilpins*. Interestingly, village art appears to have been honored alongside court art, a rarity in any imperial society. Craftsmen were organized into guilds which in turn became effective schools, where skills were passed on from one generation to the next. Each village ideally had five craftsmen: carpenter, blacksmith, potter, barber, and washerman. Although the empire did not expand its borders all the way into the peninsula, trade was extended through central India and into the south, joining in commerce previously isolated communities. There was, at this time, a widely dispersed cotton industry as well as a flourishing trade in silk, wool, gems, iron, sandalwood, and incense. Imperial administration was wisely organized, with the village as the fundamental unit. Each village had its own leader and officers to run its various functions, such as the maintenance of public pastures, forests, reservoirs, and wells, and the collection of revenue. Villages were then ideally grouped into networks of ten, then a hundred, and finally a thousand to form large political sectors. Rural India in the third century B.C. was well defined. Within an empire that encompassed many different subcultures, each village contributed materially and creatively to the whole.

By the middle of the second century B.C., the Mauryan Empire had weakened and been supplanted by the Shungas in north and central India. The Shungas were Buddhists also, but Buddhism by this time had grown more dogmatic, centered largely around relic worship. The Shungas continued to encourage artistic production to embellish Buddhist sites—the most remarkable of which were stupas, or reliquary mounds, such as those at Sanchi and Barhut, profusely decorated with sculptural motifs. These sculptures are unusual in Indian art for they primarily depict genre scenes, showing us the daily life of both court and village, and craftsmen at their work. Many of the villages shown are remarkably similar to contemporary ones. There are several styles of sculpture on each stupa, suggesting that itinerant craftsmen were brought from different areas to work on them—a strong example of the interplay between rural and urban art in historical India.

In the Deccan and the far south, small kingdoms began to gather strength in the second century B.C. Preeminent among them was that of the Satavahanas, whose reach extended from the central Deccan to the sea. By the next century they had established towns and cities throughout central and much of southern India and had founded a network of ports along both coasts. From the other side of the Indian Ocean, Arab fishing boats were occasionally blown off course as far as India. Over a period of centuries, they learned to navigate the Indian Ocean by harnessing the power of the great seasonal winds, the monsoons. With the extension of this knowledge into commercial shipping, the coastal ports were opened to Roman trade on the west and Chinese (Han) trade on the east. These ports were nuclei for trade, with textiles, metal goods, jewels, ivory, woods, perfumes, and spices brought to them from inland villages. The togas of Rome were made of Indian cotton. In fact, historians consider the huge

The coast of Karnataka, stretching for 150 miles, is separated from the rest of the state by the same mountain range, the Western Ghats, that isolates Kerala from the rest of India. The large wooden sailing vessels used in fishing villages, such as this one near Honavar, are stylistically reminiscent of the Arabian dhows that began trading here before the time of Christ.

Many of the ports where Europe and Asia historically traded—Bombay, Cochin, Madras, Vishakhapatnam, and Calcutta, among others—are still centers of mercantile activity. Stretched between these ports are countless fishing villages whose inhabitants still spend their days pursuing the age-old profession of fishing. Fisherwomen in contemporary Maharashtra hang fresh fish to dry on bamboo racks prior to their being shipped to urban and inland markets. (Thul, Kolaba District)

quantities of gold sent from Rome to India to pay for these luxuries during the next few centuries as one of the main drains on the capital of the Roman Empire resulting in its dissolution. In India, it was a period of affluence; villages were well organized and rural products in full demand. Artistry was still at its height, particularly refined in the continued carving at Sanchi and the monumental cave temples and monasteries at Ajanta and Ellora.

A second great assimilation in India occurred during the first two and a half centuries of the Christian Era in the West. Small kingdoms were consolidating in the far south. The Satavahanas continued their empire in the Deccan, while the Shakas, a group of Mongolian invaders, controlled a section of the northwestern coast. The Kushanas, a western Asian empire, extended their borders into contemporary Afghanistan and Punjab (including territories occupied by the descendents of the Greeks left by Alexander) and into the Gangetic Plain, supplanting the Shungas. At this time, most of Eurasia was governed by four great empires: the Roman, Parthian (descended from the Greek Empire, which had retained a large section of Persia and Mesopotamia), Kushana, and Han (Chinese) in the Far East. The Romans and the Parthians were enemies, and the Kushanas acted as a pivotal buffer between them and as middlemen, by sea and land, between China and Rome. The Kushanas controlled the fabled Silk Route, extracting heavy revenues for its maintenance and encouraging trade both east and west. Villages throughout India, at this time, supplied goods to foreign markets (Roman coins and beads have been found far inland). All of this

movement in commerce and political boundaries had an inevitable impact upon the cultures of India. Knowledge was exchanged, and with it technologies, customs, and styles. The full significance of these new ideas upon Indian villages is difficult to gauge, but it must be deduced that numerous rural adaptations resulted. In art, for instance, exquisite stone and clay sculptures were made in the north in a style reminiscent of Greek artistry, while terracottas in the Deccan from this period have a distinctly Roman cast. With the passage of centuries, these distinct sculptural styles, like other forms of foreign influence, were adapted and modified to become part of the mainstream of Indian culture.

The fourth to the seventh centuries saw a great revival of Indian cultural pride and indigenous leadership. The Gupta Dynasty, newly based in the Gangetic Plain, introduced India's Classical Period. After centuries of first Buddhist, and then foreign, rule, northern India delighted in the resurgence of Hinduism. As a result of court patronage in many spheres, a rich diversity of ideas and approaches was synthesized, producing refinements in all the arts and in literature. Concepts of fair administration, legislation, and social order were finely honed and implemented. The momentum created by this new high idealism and its numerous practical achievements spread throughout the subcontinent, causing spectacular developments in every field. Hinduism saw within it the popular rise of a new cult, Bhakti ("devotion"), which emphasized a personal relationship with one's god and postulated the possibility of liberation from rebirth through intense faith. The accomplishments of the Gupta Dynasty in the areas of religion, philosophy, science, astronomy, mathematics, and the arts proved a lasting legacy to world progress.

Trade with the West decreased severely as a result of the weakening of the Roman Empire in the fourth century. In China, however, Buddhism had become the imperial religion, causing increased interest in India, both for purposes of trade and for religious pilgrimages. Between A.D. 399 and 695, Chinese Buddhists traveled throughout most of India, covering extensive areas of the interior. They kept detailed accounts of their journeys, providing descriptions of both urban and rural communities. Many land reforms, including a new concept of land ownership, evolved in the Classical Period. With the revival of Hinduism, Indian society became temple oriented much as European society would become church oriented during the Middle Ages and the Renaissance. As described in the Chinese accounts, land around a town or village was owned by the main temple or by various smaller temples, and villagers worked it on a tenant-farmer basis. A similar situation exists in many parts of India today. Brahmanical hierarchy became firmly established as Brahmans held the only keys to formal worship and a greater overall emphasis was placed on purity of caste. Within Hinduism Bhakti continued as an important cult as did Tantra: the devotion to Shakti, or feminine energy, combined with an overlay of esoteric eroticism. Thirty-two craft manuals, the *Shilpashastras*, were written by Brahmans early in the fifth century, establishing ethics of design and prescribing a specific social order for craftsmen. As temples commissioned more artwork, artisan guilds flourished. As always in India, itinerant craftsmen and laborers came from villages, often distant, to complete these commissions. Thus, with demands from both the interior and from east Asian trade, and with new encouragement to produce indigenous designs to enhance India's image, villages in the third to seventh centuries prospered.

The next few centuries are referred to as India's Medieval Period. The larger empires which attempted to embrace all of India had broken up. In their place grew numerous smaller empires and kingdoms. The only exception to this was in the far south, where, under the Pallavas, the Pandyas, and the early Cholas, an indigenous Classical Period flourished until well into the seventeenth century, encouraging the expansion of Hindu culture and its sensitive expression in all fields. In the Deccan and the north, however, the cultures seemed to have lost some of their vitality. Hinduism had replaced Buddhism in almost all areas of India, except for Bengal, by the seventh century. The artisan guilds, so pervasive in earlier centuries, had lost their dominant position everywhere but in the far south (where, in some disciplines, they still flourish). The sixth through the eighth centuries saw the growth of the Indian landed classes, the Brahmans and Kshatriyas, who moved away from the cities to manage farmlands and oversee rural production. Villages were organized in much the way they are today. Each had a headman, or *thakur*, who acted as the leader of the locally appointed village assembly, known as the *panchayat*. Each villager was expected to provide his landlord with some free labor and between one sixth to one third of his crop or craft

Religion in India merges past with present. Hindus believe they acquire merit with the gods by going on pilgrimage, often traveling great distances by bus, train, cart, and foot to visit ancient temples and holy sites. The farmer shown here has traveled over two hundred miles from his village to visit this temple, which was carved out of solid rock and dedicated to Shiva in the sixth century. (Badami, Bijapur District, Karnataka)

There is evidence to suggest that bullocks have been used by Indian farmers to till their fields for millennia. In an over-populated society, in which individual plots of land tend to be small, bullocks can be more effective than costly tractors. Agrarian modernization usually takes the form of metal blades for plows and metal axles for carts. (Bankut, Varanasi District, Uttar Pradesh)

output. The nurturing and cultivation of new and better crop strains—including fibers for weaving, dye-producing plants, aromatics, spices, medicinal herbs, fruits, and vegetables—were approached scientifically. If a village shrine was large or sufficiently important, it would attract Brahmans as priests and administrators. Smaller shrines, and there were usually six or more in each village, were tended by non-Brahman members of the local priestly caste. By this time, orthodox Hinduism had a strong hold throughout rural India. Village gods, usually derived from individual local legends, were reclassified as incarnations of the principal Hindu gods, thereby providing a common ground for Hindus from otherwise very different cultures.

In A.D. 632 Mohammed The Prophet died in Arabia. The freshness of his revelations resulted in the rapid expansion of Islam. By 712, Arabs had conquered the Sind, in what is now southern Pakistan. They were unable to extend their boundaries farther into northern India, but, nevertheless, over a period of four centuries, they caused considerable damage and a great loss of wealth through the regular raids they conducted in northern Hindu kingdoms. Also during this time, while the far south continued in its Classical Period, the Deccan as well as central and northern India were divided both internally and from one another by opposing powers. India's contact with Europe was now almost entirely through the Arabs. Thus, inevitably, exports were greatly reduced. Trade with China also declined.

This gradual weakening of indigenous political powers in northern India invited powerful military thrusts in the eleventh and twelfth centuries by Muslim Turks, who had settled in Afghanistan. Their encroachments extended farther and farther into the Gangetic Plain until, by 1196, one of these groups, the Ghurids, captured Delhi (now India's capital and a centrally administered territory near the northwestern border of Uttar Pradesh). They established the Delhi Sultanate, a military governorship of northern India that existed from the thirteenth until the sixteenth century and was loosely bound to the Caliphate and to the Ottoman Empire in Constantinople. The Islamic Empire at this time extended from Delhi to Spain, with numerous sultanates, smaller empires, and feudal states established to administer it. Because believers were free to travel at will anywhere in Muslim territory, Delhi quickly filled with an odd mixture of foreigners. In response to different factions within the constantly changing populace, the leadership of the Sultanate was replaced frequently during those three and a half centuries. The country's borders also fluctuated—at times extending far into the peninsula, at others constricting due to military reprisals by the Hindus—depending on the strength of any given administration. With so many extraneous influences in northern India, this was a period of tremendous cultural exchange. Many Hindus and Buddhists, their self-esteem weakened as a result of invasion and pressured by their Muslim conquerors, converted to Islam, convinced that it offered them more opportunities. Most who converted were from the lower classes, especially artisans, but even though the number of converts was large, the proportion was still relatively small

Opposite: The ancient shrine of Gurushikhara, carved out of
solid rock at the summit of Mount Abu, Rajasthan's tallest peak
(5,650 feet), is believed by many Hindus to be the center of the
universe, synonymous with Mount Kailasha, the mythological
home of the gods. Tended by local Brahmans, it is a focal point
for pilgrimages from all over India.

Above: The ruins of ancient structures are scattered throughout
the Indian countryside, tangible reminders of the subcontinent's
varied history. Villages and towns are built up around these
relics, and often old architectural elements are incorporated in
new houses and temples. (Badami, Bijapur District, Karnataka)

Simple villages in western Madhya Pradesh often contain architecture that suggests former wealth. On the edge of a village tank in Satna District stand two such monuments: in the foreground a *chhatri*, or ceremonial cremation platform, and in the center a small temple dedicated to Shiva, the god of creation and destruction. Although both are Hindu, they exhibit a blend of Muslim and Hindu architectural styles characteristic of the area.

The Deccan Plateau in western Karnataka is strewn with boulders. In the fourteenth century it was the center of a powerful empire, Vijayanagara, which was virtually unconquerable for two centuries. During that time the landscape shown here was covered by a vast city that equaled the size of Rome in those days. In 1565 an alliance of warring nations so leveled the city that today only scattered ruins remain at the site.

and the mass of the population remained Hindu. Earlier conquerors had not tried to change the religious orientation of the indigenous population. The Muslims, by doing so, caused great resentment among the Hindu peoples, a sentiment which remains among many even today (and which caused the twentieth-century partitioning of the subcontinent into two countries, India and Pakistan). Craftsmen, however, in both urban and rural communities, acted as unwitting liaisons between opposing cultures. Muslim cities were built, and with them palaces, mosques, and tombs, and Indian craftsmen were employed for their construction. The tradition of drawing together competent artisans and laborers from villages and towns all over India persisted, resulting in a new era of Hindus and Muslims working together. In this process, much of Hindu learning and technology was passed on to the new regime. Because borders were open, these ideas passed easily through Asia and into Europe, significantly changing European thought and contributing to the very foundations of modern science (some of the breakthroughs introduced by India include the concept of infinity, the decimal system, accurate astronomical calculations, and numerous important medicines).

In the late Middle Ages, European countries began to expand their trade in Asian goods independent of Arab and Persian middlemen. Columbus, sailing from Spain in 1492, was one of the first to try to find a sea route to India, resulting in his discovery of America. Vasco da Gama's triumphant return from India to Portugal entirely by sea in 1499, his ship laden with spices and textiles,

marked the beginning of a new era. By 1510 the Portuguese had wrested control of the Indian Ocean from the Arabs (a control which they would maintain until the early seventeenth century), and had set up a major commercial colony at Goa on India's western coast. From Goa and other ports subsequently established on the western coast (among them Daman, Mangalore, and Cochin), they were able to supply Europe with desirable Indian commodities, among them the pepper and spices used for preserving meat, and the cotton and silk which formed the cornerstone of the burgeoning fashion industry in Europe. As in earlier ages, these commodities were supplied to Indian ports through trade with interior towns and villages.

Meanwhile, the Delhi Sultanate continued to attempt expansion into the whole subcontinent. Political disagreements and personal ambition led to the founding of several independent Muslim states in central India, all of which constantly feuded with Delhi. In the southern Deccan, in 1336, the Sultanate's hopes and ambitions were finally laid to rest when the last great Hindu empire, Vijayanagara, was founded. Vijayanagara was a particularly militaristic kingdom, expanding during the fourteenth century to include most of the southern peninsula, and frequently fighting both Muslim and Hindu neighbors to keep its borders safe. Portuguese and Italian travelers in the early sixteenth century wrote detailed accounts of aspects of the Vijayanagara Empire they witnessed. According to these eyewitness accounts, Brahmans were wealthy, holding particularly important positions in government and society. Communities were still

Right: A recent government restoration project at Vijayanagara, Karnataka, has given extra employment to local villagers who work as laborers in archaeological excavations. Here, two women use a fallen column as a giant rolling pin to prepare the mortar used in reconstruction.

Opposite: Stone steps to an abandoned temple rise above the granite-lined canals and aqueducts built centuries ago to service the farms of Vijayanagara. The ancient irrigation system still functions, and, amid a barren landscape, farmers grow verdant crops of rice, bananas, and sugarcane.

organized around the temples, which owned most of the land, employed many villagers, and controlled most of the commerce. Cities and towns were well designed and agricultural lands thoughtfully laid out, with an intricate system of dams, canals, and aqueducts implemented to provide effective irrigation to otherwise dry areas. Fine craftsmanship was encouraged and towns were important as market centers for rural production. Exports to China, Ceylon, Africa, Persia, and, later, Portugal included precious woods, plain and printed cottons, dyes, spices, rice, millet, coconut, and sugar. Vijayanagara was finally conquered and destroyed by a coalition of neighboring Hindu and Muslim kingdoms in 1565.

Thirty-nine years earlier, Babur, a Turk from western Asia and a descendent of both Genghis Khan and Timur (Tamerlane), had seized Delhi from the Sultanate and with that act founded the Mughal Dynasty. Although the Mughals' position as rulers was unstable for the first thirty years of their reign, they were ultimately established as the paramount power in northern India by Babur's grandson Akbar in 1556. Akbar was a superb civil administrator, conscious of the needs of his people and competent at structuring reform. He established an organized and responsible administrative, judiciary, and financial system controlled by a clearly defined imperial hierarchy that remained effective and intact even when the empire grew to encompass most of the subcontinent. With characteristic political ingenuity, he succeeded in asserting his military might and making his kingdom virtually invincible in northern India by giving Hindu Rajput princes,

previously his antagonists, commanding positions in his military and provincial government and by marrying a series of neighboring Hindu princesses, thereby securing Hindu royal alliances and ensuring political stability. As in the days of the Sultanate, foreigners flocked into Delhi from all parts of Asia. Akbar, however, was judicious in choosing only the most intelligent, loyal, and capable men as administrators. Thirty percent of administrative jobs were given to Hindus, with few holding ranks superior to Muslims.

The heavy taxes levied by the Mughals had a most profound impact upon rural India; fully one quarter of the dynasty's income was derived from land revenue. The Mughal treasury became so wealthy under Akbar and his descendents that monumental building programs were undertaken and completed. Court-patronized crafts were unparalleled in lavishness. Architects, builders, and craftsmen were brought to Mughal cities not only from throughout India but also from other parts of Asia. Government-sponsored craft workshops were established to produce exquisite jewelry, stonecarving, metalwork, carpets, and textiles, featuring combinations of indigenous Indian and traditional Islamic designs. The Mughals employed highly specialized designers to conceive each work of art, causing for the first time in India a separation between the craftsman and his inspiration, an emphasis on the individual versus the anonymous. Akbar also ushered in a new liberalism in Muslim thought. He was learned in, and open to, Hindu and Buddhist ideologies, and he encouraged free religious and philosophical dialogues, which resulted in a

A verdant waterway typical of Kashmir.

further blending of Muslim customs with Indian tradition and the beginnings of a truly composite culture. Although Islamic influence was felt throughout most of India, its most obvious rural effects were found in villages in Uttar Pradesh, West Bengal, Gujarat, and Andhra Pradesh.

The Mughal Dynasty of the sixteenth and seventeenth centuries spurred village industry to new heights as well as laying the groundwork for its decimation. With major control of the government and of the social hierarchy in the hands of the Muslims, Hindu society was forced to become more introspective. With that introspection came an inbreeding of ideas and an overstressing of the importance of roles. The strictures of caste became inviolable, as Brahmans centered their entire attention on religious duties, citing scripture as the basis for social regimentation. The temple, which already held autonomous control of most rural lands, became the focus of Hindu society. The Bhakti cult grew in popularity, mostly among the lower castes, confirming through poetry and song the rural Hindu belief in mystical love. Guru Nanak, in the late fifteenth century, had fused the esoteric aspects of Islam, Hinduism, and Bhakti into a new philosophy, whose advocates became known as Sikhs. Sikhism, centered at the Golden Temple in Amritsar, in Punjab, stressed a casteless religious tolerance and soon became widespread throughout northwestern India, particularly in Punjab, Haryana, and Uttar Pradesh. Later, in reaction to persecution by the Mughals, the Sikhs adopted a militaristic, aggressive attitude, fashioning themselves into some of India's finest warriors. With the assimilation of Muslim ideas into Hindu culture came new social restrictions such as *purdah*, the veiling and secluding of women in the home, adopted by many Hindu villages in northern and central India. Most villages remained isolated, each producing its own food and each supporting its own craftsmen who made whatever items were needed: carpenters helped with building and made carts, plows, and tools; wheelwrights made wooden wheels; potters threw all the vessels needed for cooking and storage; smiths forged knives, metal tools, and weapons; and weavers wove the cotton or silk for clothes.

Akbar's descendents continued for half a century after his death to administer a tight empire. Boundaries were extended farther into the peninsula, and architecture and crafts continued to flourish. Aurangzeb, Akbar's great-grandson, seized control of the empire in 1659. A superb administrator, he was also a religious bigot who made fanatic attempts to restore Muslim orthodox control in India. His reign was the direct antithesis of the tolerant rule of his predecessors. Among other things, he introduced a head tax on all non-Muslims, thus alienating a large segment of the population, including all those Hindus who had served his forebears loyally. His belief that much of what was being built and made in the imperial workshops was heretical to pure Islam caused him to withdraw his patronage. In his many military campaigns, he destroyed temples and Hindu and Buddhist monuments throughout India. One of his primary objectives was to annex the central Indian autonomous Muslim states and to extend his empire to cover South Asia. Although he largely succeeded in these goals—the only exception to his dominion being a small portion of Hindu-held land in the far southwest (in present-day Kerala)—he so overextended his treasury that his subjects became impoverished. In 1690, for the first time in history, virtually all of India was held by one empire, but the new administration's intolerance and lack of foresight ultimately led to its own disintegration.

The seventeenth and eighteenth centuries in India saw numerous shifts in power and influence. With Aurangzeb's invasion, the Classical Period in the far south, under the Cholas, finally came to an end. In response to the dogmatic approach to Islam exhibited by the later Mughals, many radical Hindu factions sprang up around the subcontinent. Chief among them were the Marathas, a militant anti-Muslim group that, from within the Mughal Dynasty, gradually gained power in western India. Organized by a man named Shivaji, the Marathas continually antagonized the Mughal administration and Muslim communities, gradually winning support and spreading as far east as Bengal in 1752 and as far north as the Punjab in 1784. (Today many of the rural areas of Madhya Pradesh and Maharashtra reflect the Marathas' influence.) The Bhakti movement, too, continued to gain momentum throughout India, revealing a new political orientation as it stressed the purely indigenous aspects of common Hinduism. Nevertheless, even with these and other Hindu reactions to Muslim dominance, Hinduism in the period of Mughal disintegration was neither spiritually nor culturally as strong as it had been in earlier centuries. High taxation and overexpenditure of imperial funds for militant causes had wrought

an unstable condition throughout India in the eighteenth century and had resulted in widespread famine, misery, and disorder. The road system begun by the Mauryans, extended by subsequent empires and kingdoms, and maintained by the early Mughals had fallen into disrepair, as had water and irrigation systems everywhere. Craftsmen who had depended on imperial support were left unemployed. Villagers, whose lives had always been held in a delicate balance, with the demand for their products, their labor, or their expertise on one side, and devastation from natural causes and heavy taxes on the other, were impoverished. And, as a result of Islamic-induced Hindu introspection, the new rigidity of the caste system became almost unbearable.

Since the dissolution of the Roman Empire, India had always been wealthier than Europe, and with traders bringing back tales of the opulence of the new Mughal Dynasty, the West's interest became that much more acute. Internal political problems had weakened Portugal's hold on Indian trade, and other Europeans, anxious to avail themselves personally of India's merchandise, took advantage of the situation and, with advanced nautical techniques, established trading ports on India's coast. Queen Elizabeth had sent the first English embassies to the Mughal court before the end of the sixteenth century. The British East India Company was founded in London in 1600, and in 1612 it received permission from the Mughals to establish a port at Surat on the northwestern coast (in present-day Gujarat). By leasing factories at Madras from a Hindu prince in 1640, the English rapidly expanded their ports along both coasts during the rest of the seventeenth century, vying with their old enemies, the French, for control of southern trade. With these new ports came an increased demand for goods. As preindustrial India was still more than ninety percent rural, it was largely the village farmers and craftsmen who supplied the market. Indian wares flooded European shops and warehouses, creating fashions and changing styles in every field. Textiles were among the most important exports: chintz, calico, gingham, muslin, silk, satin, velvet, and brocade as well as quilts, embroideries, and carpets. Other important trade goods sent to Europe were jewelry; gold, silver, and brass wares; precious woods and cabinetry; and arms and armor. The detailed accounts kept by English, French, Portuguese, and Italian travelers during this period provide valuable descriptions of rural artisan communities and of their means of production.

The Mughal grip on India's administration weakened further in the eighteenth century. The small Muslim and Hindu states which rose in its stead were for the most part weak as well. The main political force was wielded by the new European mercantile companies, who competed with one another for larger shares of the Indian economy. The British East India Company, by cleverly allying itself with first one and then another susceptible ruler of a small kingdom, by focusing on neighboring jealousies and Hindu-Muslim rivalries, and by providing mercenary military assistance wherever required, was able to expand its base rapidly, so that by 1790 it had gained almost complete control of India.

The enormous wealth pouring into Britain from her colonies, with the majority of that wealth coming from India, enabled the restructuring of the whole British system. For the first time, the English could afford to patronize scientific investigation and inventiveness on a large scale, thus laying the groundwork for the Industrial Revolution, which was to have such dire consequences for both the Indian population and its economy. Until the late eighteenth century, Britain's interest in India was motivated more by the avariciousness of one private mercantile company than by any colonial ambitions. The British East India Company was careful not to interfere with religions or customs, leaving nominal political control in the hands of the princes with whom it had negotiatied treaties. It was easy to make a fortune in India, and many of the company agents were entirely unscrupulous both in their business ethics and in their private lives. Reactions in London against some of their more excessive behavior resulted in the India Act of 1784, which gave the British government full control of the company, but kept the company as a partner in all mercantile negotiations. The government appointed a Board of Control, presided over by a governor-general, to supervise all civil, military, and revenue matters in India.

By the early nineteenth century it was obvious to all that the English were the dominant power in India. For the next fifty years, the British focused their attention on gaining complete political control, so that by 1857, two thirds of India was under their direct administration, with the other third held by Indian princely states under British protection. In the 1830s, under the auspices of Governor-general

81

Hero stones are a common sight in rural Rajasthan. They were commissioned from local stonecarvers by Rajputs to commemorate the heroic deeds of their ancestors. This one, located in Udaipur District, portrays a dead warrior carrying a sword and at his side his wife, who committed ritual suicide (*suttee*) by throwing herself upon his funeral pyre.

William Bentinck, the British Indian government (which controlled that part of India under Britain's direct administration) made many administrative and cultural reforms (among the latter, the abolition of *suttee,* the ritual suicide of widows upon the death of their husbands). Bentinck, on the advice of board member Thomas Macaulay, also instituted English as the language of education and diplomacy in India, declaring the superiority of English history, language, and literature to indigenous Indian culture. Macaulay publicly ridiculed Hindu culture as "false history, false astronomy, false metaphysics which attended their false religion." In response to this prejudice, resentment reverberated throughout India to such an extent that worthwhile governmental reforms went unnoticed. Lord Dalhousie, governor-general from 1848 to 1856, expanded the system of national education (with classes conducted in English) and founded the Indian Public Works Department, which was responsible for creating a postal and telegraph service and for building new harbors and good new highways.

Hindu and Muslim antipathy toward the British, however, was not assuaged. In 1857, beginning in the northern city of Meerut (in present-day Uttar Pradesh), there was a widespread anti-English Indian revolt, called The Mutiny, which spilled much blood on both sides. The Sikhs, who had had a long history of repression and strife under the Mughals, rallied behind the British, securing a future for themselves · in the military leadership of the British Indian army. In the aftermath of the uprising, the British declared a Pax Britannica, which granted a general amnesty for those involved in The Mutiny and guaranteed to all Indians freedom from arbitrary arrest, complete religious freedom, and the right to apply for public office, regardless of race or creed. To the ruling princes it guaranteed treaties protecting them from any more territorial losses. The government of India was reorganized, dissolving all interests still held by the British East India Company and establishing a new governing council of India. The council was to be led by a viceroy, acting as the agent for Queen Victoria, and was to be comprised of fifteen British members, nine of whom would be required to live a minimum of nine years in India prior to appointment.

The attitude of the British towards India after The Mutiny was distinctly changed. The English community removed itself from all unnecessary contact with Indians, supporting only English and European cultural institutions. The government and administration were rigid and unimaginative, concerned more with the efficiency of their system than with long-range goals for social improvement. The period from 1858 until 1900 was a "golden age" for the Raj, as British India was known. Many people in England were apprehensive that Indian industry would take jobs away from English workers. As a result, a wholesale new approach was instituted, whereby India could provide only raw or component goods which would then be manufactured in Britain. For example, enormous new export duties were levied on any cotton cloth made in India, thus effectively crippling India's weaving industry while promoting English looms. Cotton was grown by Indian villagers, exported to England, where it was spun and woven, and then shipped back to be sold to

The advent of modern transportation and new roads in the
nineteenth century drastically changed the relative cultural
isolation of millions of rural Indians. Among many other groups
of people living in previously inaccessible areas were the Lohars,
the Lambadis, and the Bhils—all of western India. The Lohars,
one of whom is shown here, are the ancient iron forgers of India.
Although their numbers are much less now than historically,
they still travel from village to village by wooden cart making
tools and iron wares.

The Lambadis of northern Gujarat are closely related to those of
Karnataka and to the Banjaras of Andhra Pradesh. They are
descended from nomadic tribes, and although they remain in
villages most of the year, they still roam the desert in search of
fodder for their flocks. (Khed Brahma, Banas Kantha District)

the Indians. The consequences were both the rise of a new wealthy middle class in Britain, where there were now factory jobs for everyone, and the severe impoverishment of most Indians, who had lost a major source of revenue and were faced with massive inflation when buying English goods. New cities sprang up everywhere in India, primarily centered around the new factories and businesses charged with supplying the raw components for assembly or manufacture overseas. (Mines and refineries, metal-parts factories, and thread-making factories were just some of the businesses then dotting Indian cityscapes.) In 1885, to govern more closely the rural districts, a network of district magistrates was established throughout the country, with each magistrate in turn relying on information supplied by his own locally based network of employees. The government emphasized agricultural production. In doing so, it further removed the impetus from the village craft industry, which prior to that time had always existed as an equal economic partner to agriculture.

The late nineteenth century saw railways covering tens of thousands of miles in India and, supplementing them, an intricate road system. Having established this transportation network, the British were able to administer effectively a massive and complex Indian population with only minimal personnel. (A total of 1,000 Englishmen in the Indian civil government in the late nineteenth century controlled the lives of 221 million people.) The railroad made possible the quick supply of food and medicine to disaster areas and provided easy transportation for those embarking on Hindu

religious pilgrimages (the latter contributing to a revival of Hindu cultural pride). The new transportation network, usable in all seasons, also opened up massive new territories for settlement (in the form of both urban and farming communities), thus exposing hundreds of thousands of previously isolated villages to "modern" culture. Many of these villages were tribal, composed of people who had descended from the first pre-Indus Valley Indians and who, maintaining the core of their ancient customs, had remained resistant to Hinduism and to major change for millennia. Now, suddenly accessible to the outside world, these villages were subject to view and to change not only on the cultural front, but, in conjunction with their more prevalent Hindu counterparts, on the commercial front as well. The products of each village, formerly valued only for local consumption, were henceforth thrust into a national market; and conversely, imports were now sufficiently available to provide locally produced goods with real competition. The good roads and railways that had brought "civilization" to village India also enabled the rural population to leave it, and millions of villagers moved to the new cities for jobs.

Because of all these changes in government and in urban and rural societies, the late nineteenth century was a time of extraordinary readjustment both in terms of education and sociocultural awareness. English and European archaeological research in India as well as the study of ancient Sanskrit texts had uncovered evidence of India's classical cultures. The response among Western intellectuals was tremendous, precipitating a vogue

Living in the hilly areas of southern Rajasthan, western Madhya Pradesh, and eastern Gujarat, the Bhils are a tribe who have assimilated many Hindu customs, beliefs, and cultural values. They retain some distinctive tribal features, such as their style of dress, which is seen here on these two Rathva Bhil women from Kawant in Baroda District, Gujarat.

for the pursuit of Indian knowledge. Sanskrit and other ancient texts were translated, and numerous ancient sites excavated. Ironically, the English romanticization of India's past occurred simultaneously with an insensitivity to her present needs. But this kind of paradoxical thinking was in many ways typical. For example, at the same time that contemporary Indian crafts were being suppressed, a number of unsurpassed researches were being conducted into both the traditional craft structures of India and the processes by which crafts were made.

It is one of the ultimate ironies that English education, which had been so fervently foisted upon the Indian intelligentsia, became one of the factors responsible for bringing about the dissolution of English control. This occurred in two ways. First, European interest in ancient India influenced Indian thought as well, producing an idealized sense of the past and further resentment of Western imperialism. Second, through English literature, Western-educated Indians were taught to value democracy and freedom of culture, and so began to seek their own democratic independence. The natural outgrowth of these sentiments was the founding, in 1885, of the Indian National Congress. The original aim of this all-Indian organization was to work jointly with the English to solve problems under British rule, but within a few decades its open aim became an independent India. The new Hindu renaissance resulted in the founding of numerous societies, such as the Ramakrishna Mission and the Theosophical Society, aimed at finding a common philosophical ground between Hinduism and Western religions. These societies, too, indirectly promoted the concept of indigenous Indian cultural awareness, thereby subtly advancing the cause of independence. For most of the nineteenth century, the Muslims had entirely resisted Western ideas and learning, both because of the animosity they felt at their recent loss of supremacy and because of their religious prohibition against "infidel" education. In the 1870s and 1880s Sir Sayyid Ahmad Khan, an Indian Muslim educated at Oxford University, persuaded many other Muslims to reevaluate their prejudices and to accept Western education and modernization. He opposed the stance of the Indian National Congress, feeling that any democratic election would, of necessity, exclude minorities (Muslims in India were still only twenty-five percent of the population). In response to his educational reforms among Muslims and to his campaigning for Muslim political representation, the All-India Muslim League was founded in 1906.

After a series of natural disasters (plague, droughts, and famine) in the last decade of the nineteenth century, India fell into a financial slump from which it never completely recovered. Lord Curzon, viceroy from 1899 until 1905, instituted massive agricultural reforms designed to aid the rural economy. He also established a scheme for the protection of national historical monuments, giving further impetus to archaeological research. He was, however, unsympathetic to Indian aspirations. He seriously antagonized Indian sentiment by agreeing to the partition of Bengal for purely administrative reasons. Bengal, one of the most ancient and culturally proud societies in India, was a huge

province with large Hindu and Muslim populations. By dividing it, Curzon hoped to ease the difficulties of administration. Instead, he cut families and cohesive traditions in two and confined together in each parcel unstable and inflammatory elements. In the early 1900s there were numerous cases of Hindu-Muslim violence in both East and West Bengal—the beginnings of a conflict that would ultimately lead to the creation of East Pakistan and finally Bangladesh.

The hostilities in Bengal and the pressures exerted by both the National Congress and the Muslim League so troubled the British government that in 1909 it sanctioned the Morley-Minto Reforms. These reforms set up what was called a "Representative Government," in which the Indians would supposedly be given more say. Among the reforms introduced, Indians for the first time were allowed seats on privy councils: one seat on the viceroy's Executive Council in Delhi and two on the Executive Council in London. Indian electorates were established, organized separately by class and community, with eligibility to vote based upon income. As the viceroy ultimately had the right to veto any measure the Indians voted in, the reforms were largely ineffective. Their one important contribution, however, was to secure for the Muslims more seats in council than they had ever had before. In 1911, as a result of continued agitation on the part of the Bengalis, a new viceroy, Lord Hardinge, reunited both halves of Bengal into one province—a union it was to keep until independence in 1947, when it was divided into East Pakistan and the state of West Bengal in the newly formed nation of India.

In 1914 Mohandas K. Gandhi returned to India from East Africa after successfully leading a nonviolent movement there against racial prejudice and economic and social discrimination. By this time, the National Congress was popular all over India, but it was almost exclusively composed of middle-class Indians, who had little appreciation for the plight of the masses. Gandhi immediately allied himself with Congress, but he insisted on a broadening of its attitudes and membership to include the rural classes and the poor. He also insisted that a nonviolent approach be taken in any attempts to solve India's difficulties. His experiences overseas had provided him with a mixture of ideas springing from Hindu, Christian, and humanitarian sources. He had welded these influences into a powerful instrument for national unity that cut across caste, community, and religious boundaries. One of the basic tactical weapons he employed in his fight against the British was the ancient Hindu custom of *hartal*, or boycott, in which the daily functioning of both the administration and society was confounded by a total cessation of activity on the part of Indians throughout the country.

Earlier in 1914 Annie Besant had begun her campaign for home rule—an India governed by Indians. She was the president of the Theosophical Society, an Englishwoman who in England had fought for women's rights and in India had founded the Central Hindu College, which later became Benares Hindu University. In 1916, through Besant's influence and Gandhi's inspiration, the National Congress and the Muslim League publicly joined efforts to bring about home rule.

The next thirty years were spent in agitation towards, and the gradual acceptance by the British of, the idea of an independent India. Many thousands of Indians served the British with honor in the First World War, but the threat the war posed to Britain's stability and the collapse of the Russian Empire created serious doubts in many more educated Indian minds as to imperial infallibility. By this time the British Indian Empire had grown to its full territorial extent including, in addition to the provinces administered directly from Delhi, more than six hundred princely states, which collectively accounted for one quarter of the empire and one fifth of India's population. Borders, which in history had constantly fluctuated from regime to regime, had become fixed through treaties drawn up with each state (further stressing the unique identity of each area). In return for imperial suzerainty the British guaranteed protection and each prince was provided with personal privileges and privy purses. These princely states varied in size, from tiny principalities no bigger than an average western American ranch to those as large as a midwestern American state.

In 1919 a group of five thousand Sikhs holding a peaceful, but illegal, nationalist meeting in Amritsar were surrounded and fired upon by British soldiers under the orders of General Reginald Dyer, killing 379 and wounding 1,200. This appalling and unwarranted act shocked India and the world, changed the alliance of the Sikhs from the British to Congress, and was a major catalyst spurring Indians to rid themselves of British rule. In the same year the British government passed an act known as the Montagu-Chelmsford Reforms, which extended voting eligibility in the provinces from thirty thousand to five million. These voters, because of the increased jurisdiction of the provincial legislatures, had a voice in laws governing agriculture, education, and health. Also, of the eight members serving on the viceroy's Executive Council, three now had to be Indian.

Once Gandhi had decided that India's political goal was self-rule, he was intransigent in his insistence on all or nothing. His campaigns of passive resistance, occurring approximately ten years apart, assumed a nationwide significance as he systematically maintained the importance of joining together all peoples—rural and urban, high-caste and Untouchable—to rid India of British sovereignty. Recent sentiment, in India and in the West, has tended to make of Mahatma Gandhi a saint. Although he was indeed a visionary, his impact in the first half of the twentieth century stemmed as much from his skill as a consummate politician. His genius lay in his ability to mobilize massive public support, using religious sentiment, for a national movement based on the common man. A rare social reformer, his conviction derived from a strong sense of humanitarian ethics. He insisted on the dissolution of Untouchability and removed his own Brahmanical sacred thread (a symbolic thread placed on every Brahman boy at puberty, signifying his rebirth as a man and his initiation into the sacred Brahman caste) when he realized that the lowest castes were forbidden to wear it. Under Gandhi's encouragement, Indian women first began to take decisive roles in political and social movements. He saw industrialization and the machine age as counterproductive to India's future, and conceived his ideal society as a harmonious federation of rural democracies. In this society, the government would be decentralized, each area governed by a consensus of village *panchayats* (harking back to the traditional, pre-British council of locally elected village officials), and the economy would be sustained through a combination of agriculture and rural craft industry. He symbolized his boycott of foreign manufactured goods by learning to spin cotton thread and by wearing only handwoven cloth (called *khadi*).

Mass protests, the continual harassment and successful *hartals* led by Gandhi, and the actions of the Congress (under its new president, Jawaharlal Nehru), the League, and other agitators repeatedly impeded the administration. Aided by a sympathetic international press, the protestors finally succeeded in convincing the British government to declare, in 1935, a goal of dominion status for India. A new Government of India Act provided for a federated nation based upon a parliamentary model, with a strong central administration and increased legislative power in the hands of the provinces. The electorate was expanded to thirty-nine million voters (still only twelve percent of the population), and a new emphasis was placed on provincial constituencies. Parliamentary seats were reserved for Harijans, and equal voting rights were extended to women, with all voting still based upon property qualifications. The princes were able to nominate their own representatives and, with an aggregate

number of seats, were capable of wielding a disproportionate amount of political power. (In actuality, they procrastinated in the assumption of their legislative prerogative, Congress assumed power in their stead, and the princes lost their opportunity to be an effective part of the new administration.) Muslims were given separate seats, but too few to gain a majority vote on issues important to their welfare.

At this point, Muslim antipathy for Congress had been building for some time. Although the anger of the Muslim community in response to Curzon's partitioning of Bengal in the early 1900s had eased somewhat in the ensuing decades, and attempts had been made at a peaceable coalition between the League and Congress, hostilities soon resurfaced. In the early twentieth century, the emergence of a new Islamic consciousness throughout the world affected Indian Muslims, who were further agitated by the conquest of Turkey by Allied forces during World War I and the subsequent deposition of the Ottoman caliph. Fearing future domination by Hindus, Indian Muslims began to demand equal representation in government. As early as 1930, Sir Muhammad Iqbal, a Muslim poet, had proposed the concept of a separate Muslim nation in northwestern India (an idea which would continue to inspire Muslim imagination). Many others, however, argued for moderation. Among the latter was an influential member of the Muslim League, the sharp-witted, Westernized Muslim lawyer Muhammad Ali Jinnah, who tried to work in concert with Gandhi and Congress towards achieving compatible goals for Muslims and Hindus. When, however, specific

Block-printed cotton exported from Gujarat provided the prototype for the calico and chintz upon which European and American fashions were based for centuries. Today it is still made in Gujarati villages in the traditional way. Mordants and dyes are stamped directly onto the cloth using teak blocks carved in a variety of patterns. (Dhamacatia, Saurashtra)

Kashmir's beauty and tranquility have been famous in India for centuries—the subject of poetry, songs, and paintings. Its desirability has made it the center of almost constant dispute. A landowner's rural house displays some of the wealth of Kashmir's elite. Its stone and wood architecture is remarkably similar to that of an English country home.

requests of his on behalf of the League were ignored by Congress, and when the 1935 Act conferred upon his people inferior status in government, Jinnah, too, began to champion the separatist cause.

The elections of 1937 gave Congress a majority in all provinces except Bengal and Punjab (both of which had large Muslim populations). Congress consolidated its legislative power by maintaining control of the network of provincial ministries, administered through a central command composed of leaders drawn from all over the country. It would maintain this control for two years, until the outbreak in Europe of the Second World War.

World War II halted the evolution towards Indian independence. Viceroy Lord Wavell infuriated Indians by announcing their participation in the war without consulting them and by suspending negotiations with the princes concerning the disposition of their territories until after the war. Congress responded in protest by disbanding its provincial ministries, throwing the country's administration into chaos. The Muslim League, which had felt all along that Muslim interests had been inadequately represented by Congress, took advantage of Congress' withdrawal by aiding the British administration, and, in so doing, gained their own administrative experience. Congress refused to acknowledge that the Muslim League represented all Indian Muslims, alienating Jinnah to such an extent that in 1940 he acquiesced to League pressure and declared the League's goal to be nothing less than the formation of an independent Muslim nation of Pakistan. In the first years of the war India was little involved, but when Japan began to fight Allied forces in 1941, India became a supply center for imperial allies in the region. The Indian army expanded from 175,000 to two million, with men drawn from all parts of India, and Indian battalions served bravely on several fronts in both Europe and the Far East. Allied soldiers passed through Bombay, Calcutta, and Assam on their way to fight in Southeast Asia and China. The mass enlistment of men, the effect of contact in many areas with nonimperial foreign troops, the new mobility, and the wide-reaching mechanization and building required to supply the army, navy, and air force brought to rural India, even to some of its most remote villages, a new knowledge of modernization.

The viceroy in 1941 expanded his council to include fifteen members, eleven of whom were Indian, and in 1942 made a radical new offer of a dominion constitution to go into effect immediately upon war's end. The constitution was to be drawn up by a constituent assembly elected by central and provincial legislatures, and the right of secession from the Commonwealth was to be provided for. Party leaders were encouraged to join the viceroy's council, in which they would be treated as Cabinet members. Gandhi, in his adamant insistence on total British withdrawal from India, refused to accept this offer. A deadlock continued until the end of the war, and Gandhi and his supporters initiated a new wave of civil disobedience that resulted in many arrests, and, to his dismay, riots and much loss of life.

After the war the results of central and provincial elections made it clear that Congress represented Hindu India and that the League represented all Indian Muslims, thus suggesting that

the partitioning of the subcontinent might be a logical course of action upon independence. The British people insisted on a rapid demobilization of their army and left their government in India with little military support. In 1946 a Cabinet mission from London made a last proposal for a single, decentralized independent nation with a division of powers between both religious factions. The proposal was not accepted, and civil strife grew throughout the subcontinent. Early in 1947 a new viceroy, Lord Louis Mountbatten, was appointed and empowered to resolve the question of partition and charged with handing over full control of India to the new independent governments on August 15 of that year. Both Nehru and Jinnah accepted Mountbatten's offers on behalf of their parties (Nehru breaking with Gandhi, who believed that almost anything was preferable to partition), and the viceroy worked with charismatic brilliance and speed to implement the terms of their agreement and to negotiate the withdrawal of his British subjects.

Upon independence, the Indian subcontinent was divided into two nations—India and Pakistan. The latter was comprised of two geographically separate regions ruled by a central administration—West Pakistan, which included the Sind, half of Punjab, and several mountainous tribal states; and, more than a thousand miles away, East Pakistan, made up of the eastern half of Bengal. (West Bengal became an Indian state.) Jinnah was made the governor-general of Pakistan and Liaquat Ali Khan its first prime minister. Princely states were released from British sovereignty and all treaty obligations and were encouraged to join either nation. The

British evacuation of India was surprisingly smooth, accomplished with relatively little antagonism. (The total population of all Europeans living in India before independence was two hundred thousand.) The ensuing partitioning of northern India, however, was chaotic, with mass riots and brutal murders occurring among Hindus, Sikhs, and Muslims on both sides of the borders. Some four hundred thousand Hindus left the Sind (the area in the south of West Pakistan) and migrated into western India, principally into present-day Maharashtra and Gujarat. In the process of separating into compatible religious units, more than five and a half million people traveled in each direction across the Punjab border, where most of the violence occurred, and over a million Hindus migrated from East Bengal into West Bengal. (It should be mentioned here that the beginning of severe overpopulation in Calcutta and its rural environs dates from this latter migration.) It is estimated that a total of five hundred thousand Indians, mostly villagers, died as a result of the violence attending the partitioning of the subcontinent. In the fall of 1947 Gandhi came to Delhi and went on a prolonged hunger strike in order to effect a reconciliation between the warring factions and to stop the continuing violence. His tactic succeeded in bringing peace and accord by the first of the year, but he was shot by an extremist on January 30, 1948. His death shocked India and the world.

In the more than 150 years that Britain ruled India, the country changed radically. In 1947, the British left as a legacy one of the most extensive railway systems in the world, greatly improved roads

93

and irrigation works, and a mature administrative and legal system rarely equaled in other emerging nations. They had also developed extensive mining operations, producing large quantities of minerals (India had become the seventh-largest source of coal in the world), and had built some refineries. During the reign of the British Indian Empire, however, only two percent of the work force was involved in factory industry, and there was virtually no industry whatsoever in most rural regions. The majority of manufactures, other than local crafts, were foreign imports, mainly from Britain. Craftsmanship in many fields had ceased to be patronized, and where it existed had few foreign markets, serving a local clientele almost exclusively. Most of the country's economy had been based upon agriculture, with sixty-five percent of all Indians engaged in agrarian pursuits via a complex system of land tenure that, if anything, was strengthened by the British. Moreover, at the time India finally gained independence, it was saddled with a frighteningly rapid rate of population growth and massive urban and rural poverty. Britain's willingness to grant independence to India, therefore, was not simply motivated by either humanitarian concerns or by considerations based on mounting civil disorder. The argument for independence was ultimately waged on a much more practical level: by the early twentieth century, the British Empire's economy no longer led the world, and after two world wars its financial stability had deteriorated to such an extent that a dissenting and strife-torn India was more of a liability than an asset.

In judging contemporary Indian problems in villages as well as cities, it is important to consider several points. First, an enormous revenue had been drained from the subcontinent into Britain, especially during the eighteenth and nineteenth centuries, thus adding to an impoverishment already begun by the Mughals. Second, the population of the Indian subcontinent, which had maintained a static size of 100 million from the fourth century B.C. until the early seventeenth century A.D., had grown to 253 million in 1881, and 415 million by independence. (A major cause of this meteoric rise was the advent of Western medicine in an area where life expectancy had previously been very low.) Third, India's social and cultural systems were in many ways inhibited from natural growth, remaining in essentially feudal form, because of the continued presence of an unsympathetic foreign power.

As the aim of this chapter is to provide a context for understanding the many diverse elements existing in the villages of contemporary India, the information about the period following 1947 will be restricted to the new nation of India, which officially became a republic in 1950. By the end of 1948 the emergencies caused by partition and the consequent number of refugees were largely overcome, and Congress was in full control of the government. The two most pressing concerns facing the new nation then became the resolution of the status of the princely states and the writing and implementation of a new constitution. Of the 362 major states remaining in India, all but three joined the new nation within a few months of independence. Among them, in the west, all of the Rajput states joined together to become Rajasthan, and Baroda and the princely states in Kathiawar became Saurashtra (in present-day Gujarat). In the south, Travancore and Cochin joined to become Kerala, and Mysore was large enough to become a federated state of its own. (Later the name of Mysore State was changed to Karnataka.) Many of the princes went into public service, either civic or military (only a few, in states such as Mysore and Travancore, remaining as the nominal heads of their new states), and others went into business, but in any case their individual political powers were lost. Of the three remaining states, Junagadh (in present-day Gujarat) opted to join Pakistan, but as the small state was inside Indian territory, it was forced through military action to accede to India. Hyderabad, the largest and wealthiest princely state, was situated in the center of the southern Deccan (comprising the bulk of the present-day state of Andhra Pradesh). Its ruler, the Nizam, and his nobles were descended from the ruling family and nobility of one of the early Muslim kingdoms in the south, which had seceded from the Delhi Sultanate in the sixteenth century and from the Mughals in the eighteenth century. The people of the state, however, were eighty percent Hindu. The Nizam procrastinated in his decision to join India. The geographical position of his state, the wealth of its administration, and the Hindu majority of its population induced the new Indian government to seize Hyderabad, which became a part of the new nation in 1949. Kashmir, the last state to join India, had the opposite problem: its maharaja was a Hindu governing a largely Muslim population. He also vacillated in his decision, but under threat of a tribal Muslim invasion from

Pakistan in 1948, he quickly agreed to join India, and the Muslim invaders were halted by the Indian army before reaching Kashmir. Although Kashmir has remained a part of India since that time, its rightful allegiance is a constant point of disagreement between Pakistan and India and has been the cause of many outbreaks of hostility.

In the aftermath of partition, the country's euphoria at finally achieving independence was expressed in the first elections, in which fully one third of the population voted. The elected leaders, who by 1949 had drawn up the new constitution, led by a Harijan, B. R. Ambedkar, were conscious of trying to right many of the injustices and inequalities that had existed in India during the British regime and earlier. The new government, based in part upon the 1935 Act, was organized according to Western democratic principles: it consisted of a federal state with central and union powers derived from a Parliament, which was itself divided into two Houses, the Lok Sabha (meaning "the people") and the Rajya Sabha (meaning "the states"). The central administration was located in New Delhi, and the governing party was chosen by a majority in national elections, its members appointing a leader to be sworn into the position of prime minister by the president, who had been elected by Parliament. Villages were to be governed by their own elected *panchayats* (councils) and were required to pay land taxes to their individual state governments and income taxes to Delhi. Funda-mental rights were protected, with Untouchability abolished and discrimination by caste forbidden.

Jawaharlal Nehru was the prime minister of

India from 1950 until his death in 1964. As leader of Congress, the party whose power was virtually uncontested in its rule of India during these formative years, he was responsible for a majority of the developments that occurred in India during his tenure. He was a Socialist, but not a Marxist, who believed that the standard of living could most effectively be raised through the implementation of mechanized industry. His goal was to create a modernized, self-sufficient India within a liberated, but traditional, framework. In his attempts at achieving this goal, he fought the strictures of orthodox Hinduism as fiercely as he had struggled for independence. In his first year, Nehru began a series of Five-Year Plans, which encouraged heavy investment in both the public and private sectors and placed great emphasis on massive industrialization and increased agricultural output. The national income during his premiership rose by forty-two percent, with an income raise per capita of twenty percent. Through acts of Parliament, he improved education (although many feel he should have made it more of a priority than he did) and the rights of women.

At the time of independence, overpopulation was causing a severe land shortage. The problem was compounded by the fact that there were few opportunities for nonagricultural jobs and few unfarmed cultivatable areas still available. Although Nehru strengthened the nations's economy through industrialization, his critics believe that he did not place enough emphasis on agriculture and agrarian reform. Most of the income derived from industrial sources went into the pockets of an expanding middle class, with few benefits accruing to the rural masses. Nehru did, however, attempt to improve rural conditions through his Community Development Program, instituted in 1952, which was designed to reorganize the economic and social bases of villages and to enhance agricultural production. Villagers were given low interest credit and technical assistance, and land reforms (including the redistribution of land and the restructuring of land tenure, transferring ownership to tenants) were put into effect. Within the same program, and on a modest level, village industries were encouraged, as were education, health, and sanitation. Gandhi's ideal of an economy based upon decentralized cottage industries was superceded by Nehru's policy of large-scale industrial and mineral development. (Under Nehru, only 3.6 percent of the national budget was allocated for the former, while 17.5 percent went towards the latter.) Several governmental organizations were founded in the 1950s, however, to promote village crafts and industries. The results, especially in terms of handloom production, have been gratifying despite the lack of government priority. (The production of cotton cloth by handlooms and small factories has increased by almost six times since independence.)

In the years immediately following independence, and even given Congress' tight grip on all of India, internal factionalism was rampant. Eligibility to vote had been extended to include all Indian adults, and the effect this change wrought in rural thought was immense as the lower castes began to realize that they could at last express themselves in government. (The largest free election in the history

of mankind was held in 1951–52, when 106 million Indians voted.) For reasons of administrative convenience, the British had organized large areas of the country into provinces, based more on geographic than on natural ethnic divisions. Public clamor in modern India demanded that the new states be restructured according to major linguistic lines. (For example, four separate major languages, each representing a distinct culture, were spoken in Hyderabad, while three were spoken in the provinces of Madras and Bombay.) Under Nehru, in accordance with this desire for cultural organization, the new state of Andhra (which in 1956 was renamed Andhra Pradesh) took part of its territory from Hyderabad and part from Madras; Kerala was extended north to include Calicut (in the ancient kingdom of Malabar); Mysore expanded to become Karnataka; Maharashtra was formed from the bulk of Bombay; and Gujarat was comprised of Saurashtra and Kutch along with Bombay's northern districts.

By 1960, increased alarm about overpopulation and the lack of sufficient food resources led to new governmental programs concerning agricultural reforms. In the first of these programs financial aid was poured into specific fertile regions in order to increase the crop output by improving conditions. Nehru died in 1964, but his successor, Lal Bahadur Shastri, a staunch follower of Gandhi and a man sensitive to agrarian reform, further implemented what became known as the Green Revolution. Tube wells were sunk over the entire Gangetic Plain region (consisting of Uttar Pradesh, Bihar, and West Bengal) and much of Punjab, thereby increasing the total area under irrigation by sixty-four percent between 1950 and 1975. In the mid-1960s several strains of high-yielding hybrid wheat and rice were developed by American scientists in Mexico and found to be suitable for cultivation in India. The central government helped to finance the use of these high-yielding hybrid grains, along with chemical fertilizers, insecticides, and pesticides, and developed training programs to teach farmers how to use modern methods to best implement these products. Yields increased markedly, with the total grain production rising from 60 million tons in 1950 to 90 million tons in 1964 and 134 million tons in 1981. The population of India grew rapidly in this period as well, but, at present, because of this new approach to agriculture, there is a food surplus, with the rate of food production slightly exceeding the rate of population growth. Although agricultural modernization has for the most part benefited landowners of large and medium-sized farms, field research indicates that many small farmers in the project areas have been able to avail themselves of government aid and improve their conditions as well.

In January of 1966 Prime Minister Shastri died, and Indira Gandhi, Nehru's daughter and no relation to the Mahatma, was elected to replace him. With the exception of two years during which time the opposition party was in power, she remained in office until her assassination in 1984. Her premiership was a time of numerous crises, some of her own making, but her Congress administration also helped to ameliorate many of India's difficulties. As a leader she was both revered and strongly criticized and was one of the few world figures ever to be defeated for authoritarianism only to be reelected by an adoring majority. She was convinced of her own superiority in leadership and succeeded in retaining that position at the expense of other capable politicians. Nevertheless, she kept India unified (an enormous task in its own right) and improved the country's economy, food supply, and general standard of living. She also occupied a pivotal position in the organization of nonaligned countries, admirably furthering India's image as a mediator for world peace, especially in its capacity as the world's largest democracy.

In Mrs. Gandhi's fifteen years of premiership, perhaps her most trying problems involved factionalism, in the form of either party splits or disagreements with bordering nations. The worst of the latter occurred in 1971 when a war broke out between India and Pakistan. Earlier, in 1965, Pakistan had precipitated a short war by invading Kashmir. India had succeeded in repulsing the other nation's forces but in the peace treaty that followed had relinquished some of the mountainous territory in western Kashmir. In 1971 a general election polarized Pakistan's East and West sectors. West Pakistan voted for the reelection of Prime Minister Z. A. Bhutto while East Pakistan, with a much larger population, voted for one of its own local leaders, Sheikh Mujibhur Rahman. Rahman's policies, which included reconciliation with India, were unacceptable to West Pakistan, with the result that West Pakistan, under Bhutto's direction, retaliated violently, throwing many East Pakistanis into jail and causing nine million refugees to flood into India. Mrs. Gandhi, in response, toured Western nations attempting to raise aid for the refugees, most of whom were in West Bengal, an already over-populated state. In December war broke out between India and Pakistan on two fronts: in East Pakistan and in Kashmir. Russia supported India and China, and the United States supported Pakistan. India was the victor in only twelve days; the result of this conquest was the formation of the new nation of Bangladesh out of what had formerly been East Pakistan (West Pakistan became simply Pakistan). International aid helped to feed and shelter the refugees in West Bengal, all of whom were returned to Bangladesh by March of 1972. The war stengthened Mrs. Gandhi's position politically and, because of the power struggle that had been waged between the three superpowers and the media's coverage of the refugee emergency, the world became alerted to many of India's struggles.

National debt, caused by the war and the refugee crisis, made inflation increase rapidly. Mrs. Gandhi, who had promised in her campaigns to abolish poverty, was increasingly blamed as mounting prices, reduced trade, and rising unemployment worsened conditions throughout India. Riots and disorder threatened. At this time, in 1975, she was convicted in an Allahabad court of misusing government resources and was barred from holding office for six years. Ignoring this court order, she instead requested the president to invoke his constitutional right to declare a National Emergency, citing as his justification for this action the need of a country in peril of mass upheaval. The Emergency gave her the temporary power to abolish normal constitutional guarantees, such as freedom of speech and freedom from arrest without trial, and to establish new laws which would remain in effect for a period of six months. She used this opportunity to jail thousands of her opponents and to censure the press. Her actions were decried throughout India and abroad because of the resulting loss of liberty, numerous arrests, detention without trial, and widespread police brutality. Her son, Sanjay, an aspiring politician being groomed for premiership, incensed the Indian people even more, and set the cause of birth control back by years, when he ordered the forcible sterilization of more than eleven million villagers. India during this period could not rightly be called a democracy. The Emergency did, however, stabilize the economy and generally improve conditions. It lasted for more than a year and a half (it was reinstated two times) during which time two good harvests steadied prices, factory production and commerce increased, corruption was reduced, smugglers were jailed, and public services were improved.

When a general election was called in early 1977, many of Mrs. Gandhi's opponents, who had previously been politically incompatible, joined forces to form the new Janata party (which counted among its ranks a massive group of low-caste defectors from Congress). The Janata party's leader, Morarji Desai, a follower of Mahatma Gandhi, had earlier served with Mrs. Gandhi in Congress and had been her unsuccessful opponent in several previous elections. He became prime minister in 1977, lifted the Emergency, and, with the Janata party, tried to enact a number of reforms aimed at bettering the social and economic conditions of rural India. For ex-

ample, under his administration, most of the national budget earmarked for internal spending went to rehabilitate village industry, the second-largest allocation went to small-scale industry, and only the balance went to major industry. Once the Janata party came to power, however, its numerous internal factions proved too discordant to be effective, and few of its goals were achieved. In 1979 the government disintegrated and in the ensuing national election, to the surprise of many, Indira Gandhi was reelected. India needed a strong leader who could keep the country intact. She was charismatic, unflagging in her campaigns, and appeared somewhat chastened as a result of her deposition. In her five remaining years as prime minister she continued an administration that improved India's international financial position, increased its food supply, and helped to alleviate many of its internal problems. Conditions in rural areas are still in desperate need of attention and reform, yet numerous cultural programs inaugurated by Mrs. Gandhi have begun to give Indians a new respect for their rural heritage.

During this period a small group of Sikh extremists began agitating for the creation of a separatist state in Punjab. Their methods over a period of several years were violent, resulting in the deaths of a number of leaders of opposing Sikh groups, Hindu officials, and many Hindu and Sikh civilians. Tensions mounted when these extremists began stockpiling arms in the Golden Temple in Amritsar, the holiest of all Sikh shrines, and demanding the formation of their own state. The government under Mrs. Gandhi withheld action for

Most Indian villages have a symbiotic relationship with the towns and cities near them. Mass-produced goods are increasingly in demand in Indian villages, while urban populations rely on rural India for food and craft production. Bullock carts and those drawn by hand, loaded with rural produce, converge daily upon each urban center, and cities, such as Tamil Nadu's capital city of Madras, shown here, reflect this constantly changing interplay between the traditional and the modern.

as long as possible while deciding which of the extremists' and the Akali Dal's demands it could accede to. (The Akali Dal is the main Sikh political party, distinct from the extremists.) Finally, frustrated in her attempts at conciliation, the prime minister ordered the Indian army to surround and attack the Golden Temple in June of 1984. In the process, hundreds of Sikhs were killed and the sanctity of the shrine violated. Many moderate Sikhs felt that the temple had already been desecrated earlier by the extremists' behavior, but all were nevertheless incensed by this military action. Mrs. Gandhi's assassination on October 31 by her Sikh bodyguards was a direct result of this invasion. The pent-up anger of civilian Hindus, stemming from a resentment of the previous violence in Punjab and capped by the prime minister's assassination, erupted in reprisals throughout India and the deaths of more than a thousand Sikhs. Shortly after her death, Mrs. Gandhi's son Rajiv was appointed to replace her as prime minister (his younger brother Sanjay, who had originally been groomed for the job, was killed in an airplane accident in 1980). In the national elections that followed, Rajiv received an overwhelming majority of the vote and he remains as prime minister today.

Without question, India's most serious problem today is overpopulation. The population of India is now about 750 million, and of that total, over 80 percent are living in villages. (In the fourteen years that I have been working in India the population has grown by over two hundred million!) Recent World Bank statistics predict that, given the present rate of increase (2.2 percent per year) and even figuring in the practicable measures that could be taken to reduce that rate (considering all of the variables that make Indian society unique), controlled population growth will not be achieved in India until A.D. 2115, at which time the population will have climbed to more than one and a half billion. As mentioned earlier, government measures have ensured that the rate of food production at present exceeds that of population growth, but whether it can maintain that lead in the light of such a massive population increase is questionable.

Attention must be drawn again to the fact that historically, prior to British rule, the Indian population remained at a stationary level for over two thousand years. The causes of overpopulation are many. Chief among them are the decline in death rates due to advanced public health technology and the lack of a complementary system of birth control. Not surprisingly, in rural India population density is directly related to the earth's fertility in any given area. The highest populations and the most fertile soils are both found in Kerala and parts of Tamil Nadu in the far south, along the eastern coast (in sections of Andhra Pradesh and Orissa), and throughout the Gangetic Plain (West Bengal, Bihar, and Uttar Pradesh). In contrast, some of the desert regions of Rajasthan support populations that are only one thirtieth the size of those in West Bengal and northern Bihar, both of which are considerably smaller in area.

Considering the many other problems it has had to face, India has made remarkable progress in introducing birth control measures since independence. Family Planning, the most pervasive of all public organizations, has exerted a tremendous influence throughout the subcontinent (one finds Family Planning slogans on village walls in even the most remote areas). Rural communities are undergoing a massive change in their attitudes towards birth control. Set against this change is the traditional demand for many children—to shoulder the work load, to provide security in old age—and for a male child in particular to perform funeral rites. Added to this is the fact that birth control has traditionally been viewed as displeasing to the gods, not all that unlike the Catholic church's position as set forth in papal decrees. Beliefs such as these, especially in societies as conservative as those of Indian villages, are hard to change. In considering the startling facts of Indian overpopulation, it is appropriate to view them in a broader context. Indira Gandhi commented that a "small fraction of world population consumes the bulk of the world's production of minerals, fossil fuels, and so on. Thus …when it comes to depletion of natural resources and environmental pollution, the increase of one inhabitant in an affluent country, at his level of living, is equivalent to an increase of many Asians, Africans, or Latin Americans."

Contemporary Indian villages are the products and reflections of thousands of years of history. The capacity of Hindu culture to absorb and retain each epoch has created a unique diversity throughout the subcontinent. India's problems (poverty, over-population, illiteracy, and some extremely restrictive social customs) must be seen in relation to its positive qualities. Villages, not cities, best express those qualities. In them the majority of Indians live in peaceful, homogeneous communities, their poverty offset by a wealth of custom, ritual, and design. Their faith and the interdependence of their societies provide a unity and sense of purpose rarely experienced in the contemporary West. The last twenty years have seen a great surge of Westernization in rural India. Modernization is essential, but its most healthy expression would be a blending of traditional forms (and the wisdom gained through centuries of subtle adaptations to the environment) with innovative technologies. Just within the past five years educated Indians have begun to approach their rural societies more seriously. Departments of anthropology and folklore are opening in universities all over the country. Traditional customs and crafts are slowly being documented and supported. As it has throughout history, village India may again in the future be able to provide the answers to the demands of the greater society.

THE SOUTH

Although there are few real horses in rural India, they have been associated throughout history with royalty, honor, and military might. Terracotta horses can be found in rural shrines in most districts of the subcontinent. They are perhaps most refined in Tamil Nadu. Dedicated by individuals or whole villages to the god Ayyanar, guardian of village boundaries, and his deputies, hollow clay horses such as these are believed to serve as mounts for the gods, who ride them at night to protect each village. (Pattiamdikampatti, Thanjavur District)

The south comprises four states that are collectively different from the rest of India: Tamil Nadu, Kerala, Karnataka, and Andhra Pradesh. Southern India's topography has provided a protective environment for its peoples, enabling them to develop their cultures with relatively few intrusions. Mountain ranges across central India made passage into the south difficult for travelers and armies before the advent of modern transportation. Because of this historic isolation, the peoples of the south are culturally distinct from those living farther north, whether in the east or west. Running down the center of a large portion of the lower peninsula is an immense, dry plateau known as the Deccan. A fertile strip of land extends along the western coast, bordered on the west by the Arabian Sea and on the east by heavily forested mountains which separate it from the Deccan. Rich, verdant lands also run parallel to the eastern coast, along the Bay of Bengal, and widen out at the river deltas at the sub-continent's tip. Unlike most of India, much of the south has two monsoons a year, summer and winter. The consequent rains support semiannual harvests of rice, sugarcane, and coconuts. The western coastal mountains and lowlands have the largest rainfall in peninsular India, a condition less hospitable to rice (due to flooding) but ideal for tea, coffee, rubber, coconuts, and hardwoods. The volcanic earth of the Deccan, however, is parched. With rains from only a single monsoon and severe summer heat (temperatures frequently reach 120 degrees Fahrenheit), this area is suitable only for growing cotton, tobacco, millets, and oilseeds, and crop yields tend to be meager.

United through common linguistic and cultural roots, the peoples of the four contemporary southern states here discussed are almost all Dravidian, descendents of the pre-Aryans who originally inhabited the whole subcontinent. Dravidian languages —of which Tamil, Malayalam, Kannada, and Telugu are the primary ones—have a different base from Sanskrit, which is derived from the Indo-Aryan family, as are Latin and English. Racially, the peoples of southern India are similar to those of the north, although their skin tone is generally darker. Their isolation has not prevented a gradual assimilation of the Sanskritic concepts of orthodox Hinduism and social order. Yet southern Indians have maintained their own unique settlement patterns, kinship systems, types of food, styles of dress, local deities, and a wealth of indigenous rituals, including distinctive forms of literature, oral history, poetry, and music.

Lineage in most southern Indian villages is traced through the male, although until recently, one of the few matrilineal systems in the world existed in Kerala and parts of coastal Karnataka. Whereas most of the rest of India has a higher proportion of men than women, these four states have an equal ratio, and women here have more freedom than they do farther north. They are seen more frequently on the street, in markets, on pilgrimages, and on buses or trains, but they are still subservient. A wife is never supposed to display affection publicly and is taught to follow her husband when walking, to speak to him in public only rarely, and to eat only after the men in her family have finished. Marriage between cross-cousins (for example, in a girl's case,

105

her mother's brother's son or her father's sister's son) is preferred. Spouses are not sought far afield, and the people within a certain caste in one village are usually related to those of the same caste in all the surrounding villages.

Villages in southern India generally have wide, straight streets, with cross streets at right angles, and most houses lack the open central courtyard so common in the north. Houses are grouped close together in architectural homogeneity. Members of each caste live near each other, except for the Harijans (Untouchables), who live in their own settlements, physically segregated from the rest of the community. Traditional clothing throughout the south is unsewn. Male laborers wear a short loincloth, while higher-caste men wear a wider cloth, either a *dhoti* or a *lungi*, which hangs from the waist to the ground; men of all castes wear light shawls or towels draped over one shoulder and usually go bareheaded. Women wrap themselves in *saris*, some as long as nine yards. Unlike many women in the north, those in the south do not cover their heads, and it is considered fashionable for village women to wear garlands of flowers in their hair. Most southern Indians are strict vegetarians. The basic staple of their diet is rice, which is eaten plain, in the shape of cakes, or is ground and mixed in a batter with flour and grilled as a sort of pancake; in whatever form it is consumed, the rice dish is complemented by a variety of vegetable curries and fruits.

Southern India is still somewhat isolated. Although tourists come to Tamil Nadu to visit Madras and the temple centers, to Kerala to enjoy the beaches and wildlife preserves, to Karnataka to visit Mysore and Bangalore, and to Andhra Pradesh to see Hyderabad, there are still far fewer visitors in this area than in northern India, and few venture into rural areas. These four states are closer to the equator, so that for most of the year the temperature is hot, and the pace of life in villages is slow. While innovations are constantly being introduced, they are adopted more slowly than in the north. Southern Indians are conservative by nature, resentful of attempts by the central government and non-Dravidian elements to change their traditions, and proud of their contributions to scholarship, religion, and history as well as their ability to withstand Indo-Aryan enculturation.

Most of Tamil Nadu is a flat, fertile plain covered with a brilliant green grid of rice paddies delineated by coconut palms.

TAMIL NADU

Tamil Nadu is located at the southernmost extreme of the Indian subcontinent. Its boundaries are well defined, formed to the north by the escarpment of the Deccan Plateau, to the west by the Nilgiri Mountains, which reach as high as 8,700 feet, to the east and south by the Indian Ocean, and finally, at the southernmost tip of the subcontinent, by Cape Comorin. The plains and delta created by the Cauvery River in Tamil Nadu's central region are particularly fertile, supporting agriculture that is further supplemented by rice cultivation on both coasts. Most of the rainfall in Tamil Nadu occurs between October and January, when the rest of India is dry, but the constant heat and attendant evaporation of rivers have historically necessitated the building, maintenance, and use of reservoirs (tanks) for rural irrigation. Oilseeds, millets, and various beans and peas are harvested in the drier, unirrigated northern and western parts of the state.

Tamil Nadu has the third-highest density of population in India, the third-highest literacy rate, and a relatively high annual economic level. Its language and culture are more ancient than those of the other three southern states, its earliest literature dating from the second century B.C. In villages a high value is placed upon familiarity with ancient Tamil texts. The words and legends of Tamil saints, recorded on palm-leaf manuscripts such as the *Tirukkural* and the *Periya Purunam*, are read at gatherings by village elders, and the saints' poetry is set to local music and recited in plays. Many traditional customs that are beginning to lose ground elsewhere in India are still actively engaged in here.

Because of this pride in the maintenance of Tamil traditions, in the old way of doing things, there has been less social reorganization in this state than in some others. Despite attempts by the central government to reapportion lands and to restructure the economy of tenant farmers and laborers, much of the land in Tamil Nadu is still owned by Brahmans and temples. Religious worship is particularly fervent in Tamil Nadu (which is comparable to America's Bible Belt), and temples, usually dedicated to Shiva, maintain strict control of large regions, in some instances containing as much as six thousand acres and many villages under their jurisdiction. Villagers living on temple land traditionally worked as tenant farmers and laborers under the management of Brahmans in a system called *jajmani*. They were required to give a large proportion of their crops to the temple in return for general protection, aid in drought or disaster, and annual gifts of clothing and building materials. The Brahmans of Tamil Nadu did not originate there, but were brought to the region from the north several centuries ago and given lands and positions of authority by orthodox Hindu royalty. With them came a prescribed hierarchy which, if anything, further stratified and regimented Tamil society. Recently, land reform and the removal of a large proportion of the Brahman population to the cities has resulted in large estates being divided among village landowners. Concurrently, a new commercialism and an increased ability to reach a wider market has brought about the introduction of cash crops. Although many lands are still owned by

Brahmans and temples, villagers are paid in cash and frequently need to borrow from town moneylenders to meet their needs. The modern monetary economy has thus altered the status of most villagers, transforming them from subservient workers into massive debtors, but it has also broadened their awareness of the society at large and in doing so has enabled them to participate more fully in the politics of their own rural reform.

Historically the caste system in Tamil Nadu has been particularly stringent. Many villages have no Brahman residents, their population generally being composed of Vellayars, the main agricultural caste; artisan castes below that (metalworkers, carpenters, stonecarvers, weavers, and potters); and lower castes, whose members are employed in "polluting" occupations (barbers; toddy-tappers, men who make palm wine; and washermen among them). At the very bottom of the social scale are the Adi-Dravidas ("first Dravidians"), the Tamil name for Untouchables. Most of the members of this caste are low-paid laborers who maintain roads, help in harvesting crops, and perform the most "polluting" jobs, such as cleaning gutters and tanning leather. When serving a Brahman they are allowed to go to the back door of his compound, but are never permitted to enter the inner chambers. Brahmans may visit an Adi-Dravida settlement on business, but few have ever entered the home of an Untouchable. Recently, however, rural Tamil Nadu has been experiencing a gradual collapse of its traditional caste system. Although in villages today there are still few, if any, intercaste marriages, in general the castes mix socially, participate together

in local festivals, and at times even eat together. Adi-Dravidas farm alongside other non-Brahmans on a sharecropping basis, and some are even able to own their own land.

Each caste in a village has its own shrine, or *koil*. Malevolent spirits are believed to cause most of life's problems, serious and mundane, and rituals are performed at *koils* to propitiate these demons. Each caste has its own priests or holy men, who receive offerings on behalf of whatever deity or spirit is in their care, and perform blessings and cures. Village temples are the site where most disputes are resolved. It is considered a severe sacrilege, attended by horrifying misfortunes, to lie in the presence of a deity; therefore, by bringing a dispute into the temple precinct, both parties can be sure that an honest solution to their quarrel will be found.

The twentieth century has seen countless acts of resistance on the part of the Tamils to Brahman orthodoxy and the gradual Sanskritization of Dravidian languages and customs. It should be noted, however, that Tamil Nadu, and the south in general, has been plagued by less violence in both historical and recent disputes than have most other areas of India. Today, indigenous Tamil culture is experiencing a revival on all levels—a revival that is reinforced by the political self-awareness now extending to every village. Traditional Tamil arts and crafts are beginning to flourish again; the worship of village gods, which has often been disparaged by "progressive" society, is regaining its significance; village temples are being restored; and dance and music are again thriving.

Opposite: Tamil Nadu's two annual monsoons provide enough moisture for two rice crops. Rice sprouts are individually planted in flooded fields (paddies) and spread to form a luxuriant growth, whereupon the water level is dropped to allow the plants to mature. Here, as in all Tamil villages, women spend many arduous hours working in the fields alongside men.

Above: Villages in Tamil Nadu generally have straight streets and form a rough square. Most Tamil village houses are freestanding, but those in the foreground here are joined together to provide close yet private homes for the families of several brothers. The roofs are made of densely packed and cemented clay tiles, which were shaped and fired by the potters who occupy the dwellings. (Gudithangichavadi, South Arcot Distict)

In India gods are worshiped in many forms, ranging from the very basic to the extremely elaborate. In villages, where wealth is rare, mountains, rocks, trees, and rivers are revered as symbols of the divine. By pinching mud into three tiny cones about one inch high and adorning each cone with a spot of vermilion, the color associated with the gods and traditionally applied to sacred images, a poor Harijan family has made an image of the god Ayyanar and his consorts, whom they pray to for health and crop fertility, for use in their daily devotions at home. (Kurijipaddi, South Arcot District)

Throughout India trees are considered sanctuaries for the gods. Here, wooden cradles containing terracotta images of children have been hung from a sacred tree standing in the center of the village of Vandipalliam. The sculptures, made by a local potter, have been placed in the tree cradles as part of a ritual to ensure successful pregnancies.

Sacred imagery in terracotta is particularly refined in Tamil Nadu. This hollow image, green with lichen, is of Ayyanar and was made in the last century by potter-priests for a shrine to protect the boundaries of the remote village of Thondai-manatham in South Arcot District.

Perhaps the largest terracotta sculptures ever built in the history of mankind, these three majestic forms stand over sixteen feet high and are also dedicated to Ayyanar (elephants, like horses, are symbols of royalty and grandeur). Constructed by village potters approximately one hundred years ago, each one was made in a single piece, with three-inch-thick walls, and then fired on the spot. They are located at Semakottai, a small village on a rural road near Panruti, South Arcot District, and since they are unprotected, they are in danger of being destroyed, as others like them have been.

Potters have long held a respected position in Tamil Nadu. Not only do they produce the pots, bowls, and cups used in daily life as well as special vessels integral to weddings and other rituals, but they are also skilled clay sculptors who make many types of religious images. Vaithyalinga Pathar, at the left, is a seventy-one-year-old potter in the small village of Gudithangichavadi, in South Arcot Distict. At the right is Shivakumar, an affluent city dweller who helped translate for the author. Of Vaithyalinga's large extended family only his grandnephew is learning the ancestral trade of pottery; the rest work on farms or in factories. The following plates show the production techniques Vaithyalinga uses when creating an Ayyanar horse; the whole procedure takes him fourteen days, for the horse must be built in stages, with each section given time to dry before the next one is added.

Amma, Vaithyalinga's wife, assists him when he makes one of these terracotta horses by bringing him the materials he needs, supplying him with food while he works, giving him advice concerning the horse's form, and helping to build the kiln where the horse will be fired.

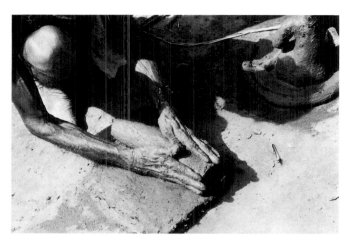

Straw and sand are added to the moist clay to make it the proper consistency.

Flat pallets of clay are then formed into cylinders on a wooden dowel.

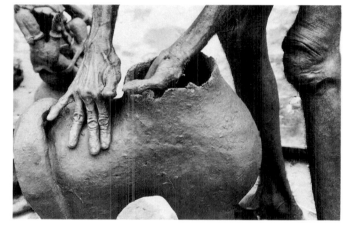

Four of these cylinders are joined to create the legs, and the horse's body is built up by adding rolls of clay that are smoothed into place.

The horse's back is carefully constructed, a tail is added, and the neck is formed.

The rider's torso is built up and his legs are added while the horse's neck is extended. Then, as Vaithyalinga waits for this last addition to dry, he adds trim.

The most difficult part of the whole construction involves the horse's head, which must be built in such a way as to prevent it from sagging while it dries; the figure's head and arms are held in place and given extra support by sticks and straw that have been added to their cores.

The most important moment, when the image is given its character, occurs on the tenth day. As he works, Vaithyalinga says "my mind thinks, my eyes see, my hands perform."

Final details are applied to the figure.

The kiln, a temporary dome made of unfired pots placed around the figure, is fueled with local materials, covered with straw and a fine layer of mud, and lit. It burns for only two and a half hours.

Vaithyalinga views his completed sculpture.

The Ayyanar horse emerging from the kiln, with legs still fiery hot. When cool it will be painted with bright colors and carried to a shrine for dedication.

Each state in India contains tribal peoples, descendents of the
original pre-Aryan inhabitants of India, who maintain an archaic
social and cultural mode of life. The Todas, one of several such
tribes living in the west of Tamil Nadu high in the Nilgiri
Mountains bordering Kerala, build unusual domed wooden
houses that have roofs of grass thatch suspended from central
ridgepoles and held in place by bamboo poles and cane. Each
house contains one room. When additional space is needed, an
unconnected similar structure is built.

The chief occupation of the Todas is raising buffalo, and it is
around this that their entire culture revolves. Compared to that
of most Indians, their pantheon is very simple. Although they do
believe in ghosts and spirits, they worship only one supreme
god. Unlike most tribal peoples, they are for the most part
vegetarians and hence do not hunt. They revere the cow buffalo
and her milk; the dairyman is their priest, and dairy and milk
vessels are regarded as especially sacred. The Todas were in
danger of extinction until as recently as a few years ago, but of
late their population seems to be recovering. This man, the
dairyman-priest of his village, is wearing the distinctive striped
Toda shawl—a garment that the tribespeople weave themselves.

Kerala, in India's southwest corner, has always been isolated from the rest of India by the Western Ghats, a band of tall mountains rising to 8,000 feet. It usually rains year-round in Kerala and the state's fertile soil yields some of the richest crops in the subcontinent. In the mountains the major crops are hardwoods (teak, ebony, mahogany, and rosewood), rubber trees, coffee, tea (still managed by British firms), and spices, such as pepper, ginger, cardamom, and turmeric, which is used in making curry. (Idikki District)

The thin strip of lowland between the mountains and the sea is 350 miles long and varies in width from 20 to 60 miles. Although the constant rains are not ideal for rice cultivation, which thrives best in climates where there is a dry season, such as in Tamil Nadu, rice is nevertheless a principal crop of this region, as are tapioca, coconuts, bananas, mangos, and jackfruit. (Trivandrum District)

KERALA

Villagers in Kerala say that their land was created by Parashurama, a war-mongering god (one of Vishnu's incarnations) who was persuaded to change his violent nature and so throw his ax aside. His gesture was considered so noble and generous that, according to lore, when his ax fell from heaven and landed in southern India it sprouted into the verdant Malabar Coast. The geographical barriers which isolate the narrow strip of Kerala from the rest of India have enabled its people to develop a distinct culture. The only traditional land access to the state was through the narrow Palghat Gap, high in the mountains, or via Cape Comorin at India's tip. The Malabar Coast was the one area of the subcontinent that the Mughals were unable to conquer. Of all the great empires of India, only the British finally succeeded in bringing this area under political control. The state of Kerala was created in 1956 by joining together the ancient kingdoms of Travancore, Cochin, and Malabar (the latter under the British had become a part of the province of Madras). Although isolated by land, Kerala had been an open port for foreign trade for thousands of years. Among those who traveled there were the Phoenicians, Greeks, Romans, Arabs, and Chinese. Elements from these foreign cultures were adapted by the entire society, in both urban and rural areas, making the state that much more distinct from the rest of the Indian subcontinent.

The people of Kerala are called Malayalis, named for their Dravidian native tongue, Malayalam. Until recently many Malayali castes were organized along matrilineal lines—an extremely rare occurrence. The most unusual of these matrilineal systems existed among the Nayars, the principal non-Brahman landowners in the state. All the Nayar women of an extended family lived from birth until death in one huge house, called a *tarawad*. Girls were married at puberty, but remained in the *tarawad* separate from their husbands (most Nayar men were trained as soldiers) and were allowed nocturnal visits from other men. Their offspring were given the name of the *tarawad* and of the mother's principal ancestress. Because of changes in the rural economy and in cultural values and a new law stipulating that children must inherit property through the father, this traditional matrilineal system has all but been eradicated. Only five percent of Nayar women now live in matrilineal *tarawads*, but since Kerala has fewer males than females, the feminine influence is still very strong in this region.

In the past caste strictures were more rigid in Kerala than in any other state. The concept of caste pollution was so inflexible, in fact, that lower-caste members were not allowed within a certain distance of the higher castes (the lower the caste, the greater the distance prescribed). Untouchables could not even cross certain bridges, for fear that they would contaminate the bridge and those who walked on it, and consequently had to walk miles out of their way. In reaction to the inequality of this system, Kerala became the first government in the world to elect a Communist administration voluntarily (since that time it has been voted out, in, and out again). The Communist government was responsible for a

121

massive reparceling of the land, distributing ownership among rural peoples more equally; for widespread technical improvements (most villages now have electricity); and for educational reforms. Kerala has always had a higher literacy rate than the rest of India. Today more than sixty percent of the population is literate (a high percentage for any Asian country) and nine out of ten children attend school.

The state's biggest problem is overpopulation. Kerala has the densest population in India: over twenty-eight million people live in an area about half the size of Maine (which has a population of one and a quarter million), but the high level of education and the basic open-mindedness of the Malayalis have helped to effect a twenty-five percent drop in the birthrate. Overpopulation, the existence of numerous universities, and the general lack of factories have resulted in overqualification and unemployment. Many Malayalis take jobs in northern India, Kuwait, or Singapore, but almost all of them return home. The revenue derived from these foreign sojourns is gradually improving Kerala's overall economy, and social and cultural patterns are beginning to change as a result. Women trained as nurses take jobs in hospitals and clinics all over India, jobs that purity-conscious Hindus from other areas would not even consider. Eighty-four percent of Kerala's people live in villages that are widely scattered amidst dense foliage (a setup that tends to belie the true extent of the region's overpopulation). There are few villages in the accepted sense of the word. Most houses are spread out rather than grouped, and in those few instances where they are grouped, tend to form only tiny clusters. Villages in this state are more rightly considered as cultural units rather than as spatially defined entities.

Kerala's unusual history has provided for a degree of religious diversification unknown in other parts of India. Saint Thomas the Apostle is believed to have come to Kerala in A.D. 52 and started the first Christian colony. In A.D. 190 Syrian Christians from Alexandria founded their own settlements along the coast. They adapted themselves to the caste system and were well accepted by the Malayalis. The Portuguese established trade with Kerala in the sixteenth century, but their form of Christianity was less tolerant. Although they succeeded in converting many Hindus to Christianity, their strong-arm tactics were greatly resented. Within the last two centuries Western missionaries have had a strong influence, and today over twenty-one percent of the state is comprised of Christians, many of whom live in villages. Jews immigrated to Kerala as well. The first, arriving in about A.D. 72, intermarried with the local population; their descendents are now known locally as "Black Jews." Another wave of Jewish refugees, who came from Spain in the fifteenth century, was given protection and a land grant by the Maharaja of Cochin. As they did not intermarry, their descendents are known as "White Jews." Mostly living in and around the city of Cochin, neither group can rightly be classified as rural, but their presence is an indication of the religious tolerance characteristic of Kerala.

Hinduism still accounts for sixty-two percent of

the population and is a major force in contemporary villages. As elsewhere, the deities and religious rituals vary from community to community. Prevalent are the worship of the goddess Bhagavati, protector of the shore, and of Ayyappan, also called Shasta, a warrior god very similar to Ayyanar, the guardian of village boundaries who defends against demons and curses. Forest shrines dedicated to snake spirits, Nagas, are popular throughout Kerala and are prayed to by women to ensure fertility. In these shrines, the multiple roots of banyan trees are clustered with the stone, metal, and clay images of snakes which have been given by devotees over a period of centuries.

Opposite: Wild elephants, rare elsewhere in India, are indigenous to Kerala's mountainous jungle regions, such as the Periyar Forest in Idikki District. Tame elephants constitute a primary labor force in the state. Used to pick up massive logs, they serve a similar function to bulldozers and cranes in construction work.

Above: As elsewhere in rural India, houses are constructed of local materials well suited to the climate. The walls of these two farmhouses are made of woven mats tied to bamboo frames. The thatched roofs, steeply pitched to maximize rain runoff, are supported by beams that fan out from a central ridgepole. Typical of the architecture of Kerala, and reminiscent of Chinese pagodas, the ends of the roofs are raised and kept open to provide ventilation. (Kottayam District)

Above: As recently as a hundred years ago, there were no roads at all in most of this state. Water is so abundant, and there are so many rivers, lakes, and man-made canals, that to this day most travel in Kerala is by water. Land is divided into small parcels, each with a dwelling on it, and, as bridges are infrequent, villagers must cross the waterways either by wading or by ferry. (near Alleppey, Kottayam District)

Right: The pace is slow on the inland waterways, whose banks are lined with coconut palms and occasional farms. The tranquility belies the fact that Kerala is one of India's busiest states. (Quilon District)

Opposite, above: The spices, ivory, precious woods, and perfumes of Malabar (the original name of most of present-day Kerala), were famed throughout the ancient world, and foreign traders who ventured here left their mark on the land. It is said that the thatched roofs and square sails of *wallams,* the wooden boats that ply these waters, were derived from Chinese junks. *Wallams* are made of huge teak planks stitched together with rope and sealed with pitch. The boatmen, a separate caste, propel their crafts with long poles.

Opposite, below: While a boatman generally owns or leases land on which his family lives, he himself spends most of his time with male coworkers aboard his *wallam.* Between the decks, which carry loads of coconuts, bananas, and wood, is a small hut where he cooks and sleeps.

Opposite: Although Kerala has historically been separated from the rest of India, it has had a constant relationship by sea with Europe and Asia since at least the time of Solomon. Many of Kerala's practices are said to come from the Far East, among them the traditional fishing technique used along the state's Malabar Coast. Huge nets are supported on stationary wooden frames, which are then cantilevered into the sea to scoop up fish. (near Cochin, Ernakulam District)

Right: An apsidal temple in Kozhikode District, dedicated to the Shaivite goddess Bhagavati, protector of the coastline, displays the pagoda-like roofline common to Kerala. Most temples in this state, unlike those elsewhere in India, are wooden. The central shrine of this one is a two-story structure that stands in a courtyard and is surrounded by a pillared verandah. Brahman priests circumambulate the temple morning and evening chanting prayers.

Below, left: In contrast to the apsidal temple, this small modern Shaivite shrine in a rural area of Kottayam District is fancifully designed and decorated to appeal to the gods. The pillar (*sthamba*) in the foreground represents the axis of the earth in relation to the heavens.

Below, right: These brightly painted terracotta figures of Kali, the goddess of destruction, are dedicated to a temple in Pulikurchi, south of Trivandrum. Villagers commissioned a local potter to make the three-foot-high images to give to the goddess in return for her protection against evil spirits.

Rice and millets are the two staple food crops of Karnataka. Most of the state's rice is grown along the western coast, where the rainfall can be as much as two hundred inches per year, the heaviest in peninsular India. Rice paddies, which must be flat with small mud walls to retain water, are terraced to conform to the slope. (near Jalsur, South Kanara District)

Villages in the dense mountain rainforests are generally aggregates of several tiny hamlets and isolated farmhouses. These farmhouses tend to be large and are built of blocks of red laterite, a soft local soil that hardens when exposed to air. The roofs are composed of locally fired interlocking tiles supported on bamboo frames. (Kudigundi, North Kanara District)

KARNATAKA

The people of Karnataka are known as Kannadigas, those who speak the language Kannada. Like the Tamils, the Kannadigas are proud of their Dravidian heritage, which has withstood the onslaught of numerous foreign occupations. Karnataka was part of the Mauryan Empire in the fourth century B.C.; Gupta emperor, Chandragupta Maurya, retreated there eight hundred years later; Muslim armies invaded the state beginning in the thirteenth century, later establishing small kingdoms in the northern districts; and two Muslim generals, Haider Ali and his son, Tipu Sultan, ruled the entire state for part of the eighteenth century. All of these foreign influences affected the indigenous culture, without radically altering it. Many Hindu kingdoms followed. Rich and illustrious, they left numerous lasting monuments to creativity. The princely state of Mysore, which became Karnataka after independence in 1947, was one of India's most progressive states, promoting public works, industry, and widespread irrigation. Rural Kannadigas are aware of their history and are proud of their achievements.

Karnataka is roughly the size of New England. It is the site of some of the world's earliest geological formations. Most of the state is covered by the vast Deccan Plateau, which in this particular region is characterized by heavy black soil that has a large lava content, scrub brush, and short grass. The soil is difficult to cultivate: when dry, it is as hard as rock; when wet, it is the consistency of glue. The principal crops raised here are cotton, millets, oilseeds, and peanuts. In most Deccani villages, families own several small plots of land (generally of varying degrees of productivity), so that they can harvest two or three crops each year. Much of the eastern Deccan, however, has infertile red soil and so little rain that farmers can eke out only one meager crop per year. In sharp contrast to this area, and separated from it by a range of mountains, the Western Ghats, is the fertile western coast, which is similar in topography and productivity to Kerala.

The Kannadigas have provided sanctuary for numerous religious sects throughout the ages, and the relative harmony in which these sects have coexisted is a testament to the strength of Kannadigan society. The followers of Mahavira, the Jains, had arrived in Karnataka by the fourth century B.C. They succeeded in converting several ruling dynasties to their beliefs, and Karnataka remains the principal center of Jainism in India, containing a large rural Jain population in the west. Jains believe that all matter is animate and go to great lengths to keep from taking life in any form, whether plant or animal. All Jains are strict vegetarians, and some even go to the extent of wearing cloth masks over their mouths so as not to harm microorganisms while breathing. Jain villagers are restrained, austere, and highly literate. Among the other religious sects populating this state are the Kodavas, a rural people living in Coorg towards the west who are ethnically distinct and have their own dialect and social customs (the latter allowing for the eating of pork and the drinking of alcohol as well as for the remarriage of widows). The Lingayats, widespread throughout the state, are members of a group

Houses in the village of Hitlalli, near Sirsi, North Kanara District, share common walls of laterite, mud, and dung and are built with heavy rainfall in mind. Not only are they raised above ground on stone foundations, but their verandahs are enclosed and can be reached only by steps leading from the street.

In Mysore District, east of the coastal mountains, villages have adapted to a much drier climate. In the middle of the day, when it is too hot to work in the fields, family activity is confined to raised verandahs. There children play, men sharpen and repair their tools, eat, and rest, and women watch their children, prepare food, and gossip across the street.

founded in the twelfth century as a reaction against Hindu religious and social dogmas. Traditionally Lingayats have eschewed caste distinctions, image worship, sacrificial offerings, pilgrimages, and cremation and have taught the equality of women. Southwestern coastal Karnataka is inhabited by the Tuluvars, more than a million culturally distinct people speaking their own language, Tulu (which has inspired virtually no literature). They live within a matrilineal social system similar to that of the Nayars in Kerala. The Tuluvars are Hindus who believe that the majority of their difficulties stem from demons and the ghosts of ancestors. Their rituals include bizarre costumed dances aimed at propitiating these evil spirits.

Today, as in Tamil Nadu, there is a certain amount of antagonism on the part of the common man towards the Brahmans. Brahmans are still the most highly educated and politically active group in Karnataka. Villages in this state are generally small and spread out. The population of Karnataka is approximately forty-one million, and ninety-three percent of all villages have fewer than one thousand inhabitants. Highways throughout the state are good and public transport efficient, but many villages are entirely isolated from public roads and can only be reached on foot. Villages are generally under the direct administration of a *patel*, or headman, who collects taxes for the central and state governments and keeps a portion thereof for his salary. Priests, both Brahman and non-Brahman (the latter referred to locally as Gudda), are cared for by the village and paid with portions of local crops. Craftsmen (such as potters, smiths, carpenters, and weavers) and people providing services (such as barbers and washermen) are also paid in fixed amounts of grain and vegetables. Landlords (from the privileged Gauda caste) expect their tenant farmers to pay their rent in grain and usually require between one half and one third of their tenants' harvests.

Traditional forms of entertainment predominate in rural Karnataka. Wrestling pits, where young men compete in games of strength and agility, are a focal point of many villages. Youths regularly practice lifting large stones to prepare for local and intervillage contests. Drama troupes tour rural areas giving what are called *yakshagana* performances. For these, a tent is set up at the edge of a village and, after dark, the inhabitants are treated to a sumptuous reenactment of one of their local legends. The richly dressed *yakshagana* actors render caricatures of dramatic heroes and buffoons, sing, dance, and recite their lines until dawn, holding their audience in rapt attention. Shadow plays, called *pavai kuthu*, are another type of popular village theater. Itinerant puppeteers cut small figures out of thin buffalo leather, paint them to resemble gods, demons, and heroes, and mount them on sticks. Backlit by lamps, the transparent puppets throw colorful shadows on a suspended sheet as they are made to dance, play, argue, and fight. In addition to providing secular village entertainment, *pavai kuthu* plays are also employed in a religious context; performances are given outside Shaivite temples during spring festivals to exorcize demons.

130

Opposite, above: Village houses in the northern part of Karnataka often share common walls built of adobe-like mud and/or stone blocks. They have no windows. Roofs are flat and pierced with small holes that, when the doors are closed, provide ventilation, an escape for smoke, and partial light. Many architectural features, such as the arched doorway at the right, suggest Muslim influence. (Badami, Bijapur District)

Opposite, below left: Doors are the pride of many households in northern Karnataka and are an outward sign of prosperity. Houses are built as fortresses to protect the family and its valuables, and doors are made strong enough to withstand assaults from both human and spirit forces. Most attention is given to the lintel, which is intricately carved with auspicious signs (such as the stylized lotuses that appear here) and hung with sacred leaves intended to drive away ghosts and demons.

Above: Courtyards are centers of activity in the evenings and during the rainy season. Hidden from view in the surrounding verandah of this one are a kitchen, storage vessels, sleeping quarters, and a walled storeroom. In the foreground is an area with a mortar, where grains and spices are ground. At night, as indicated by the stone trough, this central space becomes a barn. (Modura, Mysore District)

Below: In sharp contrast to the western coast, rainfall in Bijapur District, northern Karnataka, is often as little as fifteen inches per year. The area's major crops are cotton, millets, oilseeds, and peanuts. Houses, such as this one built entirely of millet straw by a Harijan farmer, are well suited to the heat and scant precipitation.

Opposite, below right: New doors, even extremely ornate ones, are bought by farmers to adorn their simple mud homes in years when the harvest has been good. The carpenter caste in Yamanur, where this workshop is located, is Muslim. In addition to supplying doors, they plan and oversee the construction of buildings. Without being able to read, write, or calculate in the traditional sense of the word, and with no modern instruments at their disposal, rural carpenters are capable of designing elaborate structures that are better suited to their environment than those conceived by formally educated architects.

Opposite, above: Clay pots are carried by potters near Mangalore in South Kanara District to sell at a weekly market. A pot fourteen inches in diameter will bring three cents. A potter's average production is about three hundred to four hundred pots a month.

Opposite, below: Coracles, one of man's earliest watercrafts, are still used in the rivers of rural Karnataka as ferries and for fishing. They are made of water-buffalo hide stretched over a framework of bamboo. (Srirangapattana, Mysore District)

A beaten brass urn, tilted and set on a mud base, is used to store millet grain. Aside from cooking and caring for their children and households, women spend hours working alongside men in the fields, especially during planting and harvesting times. (Kudigundi, North Kanara District)

The tribes of Karnataka comprise less than one half of one percent of the entire state population. Most have been assimilated by the broader Hindu culture. Descended from peoples who were forest-dwelling hunters, these Hallaki Gauda women, who consider themselves Hindu, work as laborers and are treated as Harijans (Untouchables). Their dress consists of a short cloth tied at the neck and held in place by numerous strands of blue glass beads. (Kumta, North Kanara District)

When villages are located far from a water source, families such as these will travel miles to reach a river, bringing with them their cattle, buffalo, and laundry. Men scrub their farm animals in the stream, children play, and women wash the week's clothes on the sandy edge. Colorful cotton *saris* and men's white *dhotis* are laid out on the sand to dry. In the hot season, when the river has evaporated, holes are dug in the sand until the water slowly seeps in. It is then gathered in brass jars and taken home to be used sparingly for drinking and washing. (Dharwar District)

The walls of a temple dedicated to Shantikamba, a local goddess who protects the village of Hegde in North Kanara District, portray scenes from the lives of the gods. They have been decorated using the rare technique of intaglio; the designs are etched into the red burnish, revealing the white plastered walls beneath.

Most Tuluvars, a large culturally distinct group in southwestern Karnataka, worship the goddess Bhagavati (in her destructive form) and a wide array of ghosts and demons known as Bhutas. By propitiating these evil spirits villagers believe they can avert calamity in their lives. A Tuluvar shrine in Mekke Kutte, near Udipi, contains a huge wooden image of a Bhuta under worship.

138

The people who made and worshiped these terracotta heads near Kumta in North Kanara District have long since disappeared. The original significance of the heads is unknown, and no contemporary customs include sculptures remotely like them. Possibly buried for centuries, they appear on the surface of the rainforest floor during the monsoon season, unearthed by the driving rains. Local villagers call the heads *magemuduvudu* ("coming from the earth") and believe that they are sculpted by the local Earth Goddess, Vanadurga. Although they do not worship the images, people in the vicinity believe that it is unwise to approach too close to them.

Archaeological excavations in Karnataka have yielded proof of a society based on the raising of cattle as early as 2000 B.C. Here, bullocks are covered with elaborately embroidered cloths, their horns ornamented with yarn, paper, flowers, and even balloons, during the Pongal-Shankaranti festival in mid-January at Badami, Bijapur District. The bullocks will be paraded by their owners through the village and then treated to their favorite foods.

Scraps of old shirts and *saris* are sewn into patchwork quilts by farmers' wives in Bijapur District in northern Karnataka. The abstract, cubistic designs are traditional.

Dressed as a local legendary king, a *yakshagana* actor readies himself for his stage entrance. *Yakshaganas* are melodramas based on epics and regional histories that include dance, song, tragedy, and comedy. Lasting from late at night until dawn, they are among the most popular village entertainments in Karnataka and serve to foster a sense of continuity by perpetuating ancient traditions. (South Kanara District)

Village women on pilgrimage perform a ritual to ensure fertility at a sacred spot on the Cauvery River. Singing and chanting prayers to Devi, the Mother Goddess, they dance in a circle around a fire.

The alluvial coastal region of Andhra Pradesh produces a surplus rice crop each year, ensuring a stable state economy. In this, India's largest state, the demographics of rural communities differ markedly because of pronounced variations in the geography. (Vishakhapatnam District)

Sixty-five percent of all rural houses in Andhra Pradesh have only one room, although many have secondary sheds containing kitchens. The houses of fishermen in Vishakhapatnam District on the Circar Coast are round with short mud walls and thatched roofs supported by poles similar to those used in a tepee. The interior is undivided, has almost no furniture, and serves as a living, eating, and sleeping area. Roofs are not attached to walls—a wise innovation in this hurricane-prone area—and will blow off in a storm, leaving the house intact. Made from local palm fronds, they are easily replaceable.

ANDHRA PRADESH

India's largest state, Andhra Pradesh, is naturally divided into three sections of varying topography, each a part of the Deccan Plateau. The Telangana area of the northwest has a marginally fertile red soil, where crops of millets, oilseeds, pulses (peas and beans), and tobacco are grown. An estimated twenty thousand lakes and reservoirs (tanks) exist in this area, the size of Ohio, providing for good irrigation. Rayalasima, in the southwest, is dry and rocky and has very poor soil, except in a few places where there are rich deposits of loam. This region produces only one poor crop of cotton, tobacco, maize, and some grains and vegetables per year. The average annual rainfall in both these areas is twenty inches and the temperature in the hot season often reaches 120 degrees in the shade. The coastal region, historically called the Circars, is composed of two broad alluvial plains fed by the Godavari and Krishna rivers. In this area, the rainfall from biannual monsoons and fertile soil enable farmers to grow substantial quantities of tobacco as well as one of India's richest rice crops.

Andhra Pradesh was the first state in independent India to insist upon the redrawing of its boundaries to reflect linguistic, rather than geographic, considerations. Organized accordingly to encompass all those people speaking Telugu—the original language and culture of this area—the new state was expanded to include the princely state of Hyderabad (approximately the size of Kansas) as well as certain areas of the British province of Madras. Hyderabad had been the largest and wealthiest

princely state in India. Its ruler, the Nizam (reputed to be the richest man in the world), was Muslim and was flanked in his capital city of Hyderabad by an Urdu-speaking Muslim elite (Urdu is a Muslim language, originating in northern India). But the population of the state as a whole was eighty percent Hindu. Given such strong Muslim associations, it may seem odd that the new political entity of Andhra Pradesh should choose as its capital this same city, but it had been a wealthy and well-organized administrative center previously and as such was the most logical choice for the capital. A new emphasis, however, was now placed on the ancient language of Telugu. The Telugu peoples, as they are called, responded with a resurgence of pride in their Dravidian language, and Telugu literature, history, and folklore have burgeoned since independence. The renascence of Telugu culture has not resulted in the local resentment of encroaching Brahmanism and Sanskritization from the north, as it has in Tamil Nadu.

Although Muslims account for only seven percent of Andhra's population of fifty-eight million, centuries of Muslim rule have had a strong impact upon the evolution of contemporary rural communities and culture. As a minority among Hindus, village Muslims have adjusted to the rigid caste system and are roughly equal in social status and income to their Hindu counterparts. Because of a history of foreign influences and fluctuating borders most Andhra villagers tend to be bilingual. Almost all speak Telugu, while in central Andhra Pradesh villagers also speak Urdu; in the south they tend to be fluent in both Telugu and Tamil; in the east they

A more substantial farmer's house near Masulipatnam, Krishna District, is separated from the street by a small hedge and has a vegetable garden behind it. The rice-straw roof, held in place with ropes, is steeply inclined to drain off rainwater during the area's two monsoons. Resting on a stone foundation, the house is divided into three rooms, each delineated by freestanding mud and dung partitions that end before reaching the ceiling.

In village houses the mud floors and walls are periodically resurfaced with a wash of mud and dung to keep their appearance fresh and clean. Floors are swept twice a day. The woodwork around the doorway is regularly repainted with red earth, and white rice-paste designs are applied daily, as in Tamil Nadu, to protect the home from malignant spirits. It is the duty of each household to sweep the street bordering its property every day. (near Masulipatnam, Krishna District)

know Kannada; and in the north they often speak Marathi (the language of Maharashtra). Telugu is spoken in different dialects and forms depending upon the origin and social status of the speaker. For a villager to communicate easily with a stranger, he must first identify that person's background and adapt his conversation to fit the occasion.

Andhra Pradesh is eighty-one percent rural, and its villages or hamlets are generally located no more than three to six miles apart. Villages are relatively large: nine out of ten have at least five hundred people and one hundred houses. (Towns are defined by the Indian census as having five thousand people or more.) Although under state and federal jurisdiction, local matters in each village are presided over by a hereditary headman, or *deshmukh*, who is usually a wealthy landowner with government affiliations, and a village council, or *panchayat*. Each major caste or social division in the village is represented in the council by its leader. The *deshmukh* and *panchayat* listen to and arbitrate minor disputes and, acting as a kind of planning commission, organize community functions, orchestrate construction and maintenance of public buildings and roads, and decide how to apportion payment for such things among its residents. Within each family the eldest male is held accountable by the *panchayat* for the actions of any of his relatives. His position is respected, but rural ethics require him to be tolerant of his family's wishes.

Islamic influence in Andhra Pradesh is particularly discernible in the treatment of women, who are more protected and have less freedom of movement than they do in the other southern states.

Polygamy is an accepted practice for both Muslim and Hindu men in this state but in rural areas few men have more than one wife. Among all the castes, except for the Brahmans and the Komatis (a local caste of merchants and moneylenders), divorce and the remarriage of widows are permissible. (Widowers are allowed to remarry in all castes throughout India.)

As elsewhere, festivals provide a focal point in the lives of many villagers. Hindus in this state have as many as twenty-three annual festivals, while Muslims have seven. Among the performing arts, shadow plays have been known to exist in Andhra Pradesh as early as 200 B.C. Called *tholu bombatta*, these shadow plays employ puppets that are much larger (ranging from fourteen inches to five feet) than those popular in Karnataka and have jointed arms and legs, requiring two people to manipulate them. The story of an epic, usually the *Ramayana* (one of the great Hindu classics), is enacted over a period of nine days, from dusk until dawn. All the characters (often numbering in the hundreds) are displayed throughout the performance, pinned to a wide cloth composed of two *saris* sewn lengthwise. When the narrative song discusses any given figure, the appropriate puppet is backlit and moved. Aside from these entertainments for the entire community, every caste has its own group of itinerant actors, acrobats, storytellers, bards, magicians, palmists, and fortune-tellers who travel from village to village performing solely for their own particular social order.

Farmers from the Reddi tribe drive their bullocks home after harvesting millets. The agricultural year is demanding, and each season requires toil in the fields: tilling and preparing the soil for planting, fertilizing, planting when the first rains moisten the parched earth, weeding and separating, and finally harvesting and winnowing. When a farmer is lucky enough to own fertile, irrigated land, his work is increased by the demands of several plantings.

Two cloth dolls link hands and dance in a circle in the wind, keeping crows and other birds out of a crop of lentils. (Srikakulam District)

146

Above, left: The toddy palm is grown in India for its sap, which is tapped in much the same way that maple trees are. Slits are cut into the bark of the tree near its top, and clay pots are tied underneath to collect the dripping sap. Sugar is added to the juice while it hangs in the pot, and fermentation takes place rapidly, producing toddy, an alcoholic beverage.

Above, right: The toddy tapper belongs to the Gaondla caste, traditionally associated with this special occupation. He carries his equipment on him: a rope loop with rubber treads for climbing the steep trees, knives for trimming branches and slitting the bark, and pots for gathering the palm wine. He makes his incisions and ties his pots in the late afternoon and evening and collects the fermented toddy early the next morning.

Right: Pots of toddy, foaming in the sun, are taken to the village by cart. Alcohol is considered a pollutant by orthodox upper-caste Hindus, and consequently they regard Gaondlas as very low-caste. In Andhra the men of all castes, except Brahmans and Komatis (merchants), drink toddy, while among women its consumption is limited to those of the lower castes. (Nalgonda District)

Top: Two women carry baskets of red chilies to be sold in the weekly market at Chittivalasa, Vishakhapatnam District. The food of Andhra Pradesh has a reputation for being the hottest in India. Green and red chilies, cayenne, and pepper are used liberally in all foods. The basic diet for most villagers consists of varying amounts of millets, rice, lentils, meat, and fish (vegetarianism is not as prevalent here as it is farther south).

Center: Elsewhere in the market fisherwomen light each other's cheroots (when not lit, they are stored behind the women's ears). Tobacco is a major crop in Andhra Pradesh, and some of India's largest tobacco companies subsidize village production. Home-rolled, green tobacco cheroots are smoked and cherished by low-caste village men and women alike.

Below, left: At the same market, an Erkala woman sells baskets, fans, and mats that are made by her people to supplement their income. The Erkala are a low caste whose men traditionally hunt, using spears, arrows, snares, and traps, and keep trained dogs for tracking and whose women sing, recite legends, and read fortunes at festivals.

Below, right: Behind a used-clothes vendor in Hyderabad District a small shrine dedicated to a Muslim saint (*pir*) emphasizes the interplay between Islamic and Hindu cultures in Andhra Pradesh. Technically forbidden by their religion to paint any representations of God's creation, Muslims in rural India often circumvent this proscription, decorating their mosques, shrines, and tombs in designs distinctly influenced by local Hinduism, such as the tigers shown here, bearing banners and flanked by pots of flowers.

Traditional herbal medicine provides a viable alternative to conventional Western practices. *Ayurvedic* medicine consists of natural remedies scientifically formulated more than two thousand years ago. It is a strict discipline, requiring years of training. An *Ayurvedic* pharmacy in an Andhra village has drawers, jars, and bins full of medicinal herbs and potions. (Hyderabad District)

The Banjaras, who work on the road crews in Andhra Pradesh, are a nomadic tribe whose ancestry may be the same as that of the Gypsies. Banjara women work incredibly hard, carrying on their heads large rocks that they break into rubble with hammers and then mix with tar to create road surfaces. No matter how rugged the work, they wear their finest clothes at all times—brightly embroidered skirts and blouses, ivory bangles covering most of their arms, and heavy silver jewelry. (Medak District)

Above: Village potters work in a large courtyard behind their low-eaved, thatched houses in Salur, Vishakhapatnam District. Pots are thrown on a wheel and cut from the base, leaving large holes in their bottoms, which are then beaten into rounded shapes. When finished the rounded pot sits in a ring of straw. In an arrangement similar to that employed by other craftsmen, potters supply farmers with all the pots they need in return for a share of their crop at harvest time.

Center: Andhra Pradesh has been famous for its cotton cloth for thousands of years. Although it has limited resources in other areas, the state employs more handloom craftsmen than any other. Ikat, one of the most difficult weaving processes in the world, is still practiced in Andhra villages. The process requires that the warp, and sometimes the weft, threads be tie-dyed before being woven. Here, small boys in Pochampalli, Nalgonda District, wrap rubber cords around the weft threads to inhibit those areas from changing color when immersed in dye.

Below: When the dyeing is complete and the rubber cords have been removed, the weft threads are taken off the dyeing frame and wound on a spindle in preparation for weaving. (Pochampalli, Nalgonda District)

Gold thread to be used in the border of a village wedding *sari* is wound onto a spindle by a weaver's wife. The traditional way of making gold thread was to pull with pincers a heated gold bar through an iron hole slightly smaller than the bar's circumference, thus elongating it. The bar was then reheated, pulled through a smaller hole, and elongated again. The entire process would be repeated until the gold became a thin wire several miles long. The gold wire was then tightly wrapped around a single silk thread and wound on a spindle such as the one shown here. (Pochampalli, Nalgonda District)

A Padmasali (weaver) weaves a cotton ikat *sari*. The design on the end panel of the *sari* has been dyed prior to its placement on the loom. As each weft thread is added a wavy design is created, giving ikat its distinctive characteristic (the same technique produces watered silk). When complete the *sari* will be five and a half yards long. (Pochampalli, Nalgonda District)

THE EAST

Although Hindu culture extols the virtues of the extended family, an average of only five people live in the typical household in Uttar Pradesh. Brothers and cousins build their houses close to one another, their dwellings forming separate groupings within the village. In the evening, after the heat of the day, families join together to feed their animals, relax, and gossip. (Asarkhapur, Gorakhpur District)

The four states that comprise this section—Orissa, West Bengal, Bihar, and Uttar Pradesh—together contain most of the major alluvial plains of northern India. The Ganges, beginning in the Himalayas of Uttar Pradesh and subsequently joined by innumerable tributaries, spreads its widening course through three of these states before it reaches the Bay of Bengal. Its water is sacred to Hindus, its banks clustered with tens of thousands of temples and shrines. With its current it carries the hopes, the prayers, and, in death, the ashes of millions of Indians. Its course has altered during the millennia, and in its wake deposits of fertile soil have been left, transforming the huge Gangetic Plain into one of India's primary food-producing regions. The lowlands of the fourth state, Orissa, are also rich in alluvials, which support biannual crops of rice, and its mountains contain some of the subcontinent's major forests, an area that is also rich in mineral resources.

These four states are bounded on the north by the Himalayas, Nepal, and the northeastern states (the latter are culturally linked to Southeast Asia); on the east by the Bay of Bengal; on the south by the Deccan and the vast hilly plateau of central India; and on the west by the deserts and dry plains of Rajasthan and Haryana. Uttar Pradesh is included in this chapter, despite the similarities the western half of the state shares with Madhya Pradesh and Rajasthan, because it is part of the Gangetic Plain and because the peoples and cultures in the state's eastern half are remarkably similar to those in Bihar. All four states are divided internally: three by geography and culture and one by politics and religion.

The food-producing capacity of this fertile region is offset by its enormous, and rapidly growing, population. The four states jointly account for twenty-two percent of India's landmass but thirty-eight percent of its population. Agricultural advances made in the last two decades—the use of high-yield crop strains, better farming implements and techniques, chemical fertilizers, and many new wells and modern pumps for irrigation—have increased food production to the point where it just exceeds population growth. Help from outside specialists has been augmented by indigenous rural ingenuity. For example, Bihari farmers have recently invented an inexpensive method of tapping the water table, which is very near the surface in North Bihar, by sinking long, native-grown bamboo poles instead of steel tubes. Innovations in agrarian technology in much of eastern India exist alongside a very traditional system of land management. The relationship of tenants and laborers to landowners and merchants is still almost feudal in many areas, and although both state and central governments have targeted land reform as a priority, there has been little improvement in this area so far (with the exception of West Bengal, where reforms have been implemented).

Dense population, geographical similarity, and a shared history of cultural and social interaction have given the villages of the Gangetic Plain many qualities in common. Villages in most of eastern India are not isolated. Overpopulation has made cultivatable land invaluable and every available plot is tilled. Villages have no set pattern, but are usually organized according to social compatibility and the dictates of terrain. Generally they consist of several small clusters of houses that are less sprawling than

Most of lowland Orissa is composed of broad alluvial plains ideal for rice cultivation. The state's many rivers flood these plains during the monsoon, at which time the rice is planted. When the fields start to dry, they must be irrigated by a variety of methods; here, bamboo tubes are lowered into a canal, filled with water, and then tipped by means of counterweights into paddies requiring water.

those of the south. Most houses have courtyards around which family activity is centered, and brothers will often occupy separate small houses, while sharing a courtyard. Although this region contains the majority of India's large cities as well as its most extensive railway and road systems, the rural population is so large that, in proportion to other areas, the overall urban population is below average.

Wheat, usually eaten in the form of *chapattis* (a soft unleavened bread similar to a tortilla), is the main staple of the residents of western Uttar Pradesh, while all the rest of the villagers in eastern India depend on rice. Vegetarianism is not as widespread as it is in the south, except among the orthodox upper castes. Fish is a major dietary supplement of the peoples of Orissa and West Bengal, while those of Bihar and Uttar Pradesh eat chicken and mutton when available. Most women wear *saris*, using the endpiece to cover their heads in public. The traditional costume for men consists of a single piece of cloth wrapped around the waist (a *dhoti* or a *lungi*) or cotton pants *(pyjamas)*, usually worn with a long tunic *(kurta)*. Encroaching Westernization has made European-style pants and shirts increasingly popular for men throughout India, especially in less isolated areas.

The states of eastern India have been linked throughout history, ruled jointly by some of India's greatest kingdoms and empires. They are the lands where the epics were conceived and set, the place of origin for much of classical Hinduism, and are bound together by major achievements in art, architecture, and literature. Eastern Hindus (not including those in

western Uttar Pradesh) have been less affected by the incursions of foreign cultures than have the peoples of the west. The populace tends to be shorter and darker than most western Indians, and the qualities of intuition and aesthetics are more highly valued than those of aggression and strength. Three of the states combined—Orissa, West Bengal, and Bihar—contain just under half (seventeen million) of India's tribal population, most of whom are descended from the subcontinent's first inhabitants. These tribesmen live in regions that remain isolated because access to them is difficult and they are culturally (and often racially and linguistically) distinct from Hindus.

ORISSA

Orissa is one of India's most beautiful and least-known states, and continues to be one of its most rural. Of its twenty-nine million people only one in twelve lives in a town or city, and the state contains only four cities of over one hundred thousand inhabitants. The official language, Oriya, has a Sanskritic base, is written in an individual rounded script (which is stylistically unique in India), and has been the vehicle of an extensive literature, traditionally recorded on palm-leaf manuscripts. Orissa's literacy rate is lower than the national average, but this figure is misleading if not considered in relation to the state's unique sociocultural composition. Over one quarter of the Orissan peoples are tribal, a figure which constitutes fully fifteen percent of the total number of tribesmen living in India today. The majority of these tribes live in the mountainous regions of western Orissa. Many of the Harijans living in the lowland areas are descended from tribesmen; only recently, within the last few centuries, have they converted to Hinduism.

Mountains cover most of Orissa. The Eastern Ghats, rising to five thousand feet, are Orissa's backbone, separating the Bay of Bengal from the central Indian plateau. These mountains are cut by five large rivers, each of which has carved out wide valleys and left fertile alluvial deposits along Orissa's three hundred miles of coastal plain, making the region ideal for the cultivation of rice and jute crops. The heavily forested mountains of Orissa provide India with a major source of wood, and recently, international, national, and state speculation has resulted in the exploitation of the area's rich mineral reserves.

Its geographical position away from the hub of Indian civilization has, paradoxically, both protected and hindered Orissa's cultural growth. Orissa was one of India's first Buddhist kingdoms, successfully converting its conqueror, the Mauryan emperor Ashoka, to Buddhism in the third century B.C. and thus causing that religion's spread throughout India and Asia. Orissa's isolation, however, allowed for centuries of political independence and indigenous development free, for the most part, from foreign intervention. It was able to withstand Muslim conquest for at least three centuries longer than most of northern and central India, and was not conquered until 1568 by the Afghans and 1592 by the Mughals. Even then, the distance from Delhi, the seat of central administration, enabled the Orissans to perpetuate their local traditions until the advent of the British and the attendant massive changes of the early nineteenth century. This area, however, was still affected less by these changes than were other areas of the country, and today Orissa's insularity allows for the maintenance of unique tribal and rural Hindu societies, in which there exist an unusual amount of cultural integrity and a strong degree of conservatism with regard to social systems.

Although technically illegal in modern India, strict caste delineations are still observed in Orissa. Most villages are laid out in such a way as to physically separate the low-caste and Harijan members from the high-caste villagers. By law, schools are open to all, and children from all social strata learn and play together there; once outside,

however, caste regulations are reinforced. Other than within the schools, there is little fraternization between castes, except during certain festivities or crises (epidemics, natural disasters, etc.). Traditionally Brahmans and other high castes were the only members of society to have access to the Hindu sacred texts. Because of the rigid stratification of Orissan society, the majority were precluded from entering into this higher form of culture and instead had to fall back upon their own devices. As a result, oral traditions, the vehicle of expression for the common man, became highly refined and some of India's most beautiful poetry, songs, dramas, and dances can be found in this region.

Women in Orissa have few rights. The social system is patrilineal and, until recently, the Muslim system of *purdah* (the veiling and secluding of women) was popular in Hindu homes. Girls are trained to conform to a feminine ideal and to be decorous in their behavior—not to shout, laugh loudly, run, or ride bicycles. Women are supposed to bow their heads in modesty. Marriage with close relatives, common in the south, is infrequent in the north, and matrimony is not anticipated happily in Orissa. A woman usually leaves her home to go to a distant village, where her position remains uncertain until she produces a child. Barren women are considered inauspicious and are blamed for their fate. Orissan women undergo numerous fasts, penances, and other rituals to propitiate the gods and goddesses and thereby procure the requisite fertility. After a woman has had her first child, she is accepted and gains security in her new home. Her duty is not fulfilled, however, until she bears a son,

who will continue the family line and perform the necessary ritual functions. Upon the birth of a male child, she may gradually emerge as a dominant force in the home and family.

Magic and superstition abound in Orissa as they do elsewhere in India. Witches and sorcerers are believed in and feared; priests and magicians are required to provide talismans and potions to ward off evil spirits, to exorcize the demons of diseases and epidemics, and to provide cures. Fear of black magic causes villagers to discreetly dispose of nail and hair clippings in order to prevent their being used in spells and curses (in a manner similar to that used in voodoo). Innumerable superstitions govern a villager's every action. The following are just a sampling. It is considered inauspicious, for example, to eat food while facing west, to sleep facing west or north, or to rub one's fingernails together (the latter supposedly incites men to argue). It is agreed that bad luck will befall a woman who touches a broom with her foot or gets irritated while grinding flour, for both actions are deemed disrespectful to Shashthi, the goddess of chastity and marital purity. A pregnant woman who burns an eggplant or a coconut shell while cooking is said to cause baldness or ulcers on the head of her child. A man referring to a child as a monkey, even jokingly, is supposed to slap his own cheeks three times and rub his ears to avert calamity. Villagers are not supposed to leave their homes in groups of three (the proper procedure being to leave alone or in twos, fours, etc.), and are always to step out of the house with the right foot, while breathing through the right nostril.

The wall paintings of the coastal regions are

In the hot season, before the arrival of the rains, fields must be tilled and fertilized to prepare for the coming season. This farmer, plowing with his two water buffalo in Ganjam District, is wearing a hat, common to Orissa but unknown in the rest of peninsular India, which reflects in its shape the state's historical ties with Southeast Asia.

among the most beautiful expressions of Orissa's rich rural craft tradition. Houses are cleaned and walls resurfaced and repainted to celebrate special occasions: weddings, festivals, births, or the arrival of a special guest. Designs, called *chita* or *chitra*, are applied to the walls by a member of each family, usually a woman. A beautifully decorated house is a source of pride for the family and is believed to curry favor with the gods for the entire village. Usually painted freehand with white rice paste or commercial dyes, most designs honor Lakshmi, the goddess of the home and prosperity. Walls are also decorated for specific events such as Shashthi Puja, a ceremony aimed at ensuring the healthy growth of a child, and Manasa Vrata, a ritual performed to prevent or treat snakebites. As aspects of religious vows (*vrata* or *osha*) that are accompanied by fasting and ceremonious storytelling, *chita* are the only visual reminders of intense devotional commitment.

In the years since India gained independence many of the customs and much of the lore of Orissan villages have changed. As national media and education increasingly reach remote villages, superstitions and local rituals are slowly being replaced by modern values. Orissans, however, are justly proud of their indigenous culture. Their villages are well cared for, and in them there is relatively little hunger and disease.

A storage room for rice, vegetables, and grain behind the courtyard of a house near Gop in Puri District has a double roof: the outer one made of thatched rice-straw, the inner one of bamboo-supported mud. It serves two functions. The easily replaceable outer roof takes the brunt of storm damage and general wear and tear, leaving the inner roof sealed and intact. Also, the air pocket between the two greatly improves insulation, keeping vegetables and milk products that much cooler in the hot season.

Opposite, above: The houses of the families of three Goala Behera (farmer) brothers in Puri District are joined by common walls and one long verandah. Inside, sleeping and storage rooms radiate from three separate courtyards. The exterior mud and dung walls have been decorated with white rice-paste designs to honor Shashthi, a powerful goddess associated with chastity, marital purity, and the welfare of children.

Opposite, below: The streets of Orissan villages are usually aligned on an east-west axis and intersected by smaller lanes branching off intermittently at right angles. The roofs of most village houses are thatched; a more substantial structure with a tile roof implies a wealthy home or a government building, such as the post office in the right-hand corner. In this village of Dhunlo in southern Puri District rice and grain are stored within earthen mounds in the street in front of each house as a preventive measure against rats.

Above: In Khonanta Kumbharsai, a potters' village in southern Puri District, walls are actually made of stacked clay pots bonded with mud. The terracotta walls provide remarkably effective insulation during the hot season and, when broken inside, double as storage niches.

Right: Brassware is a symbol of prosperity in Indian villages and is the only substance in which Brahmans may cook. A completed brass pot stands in front of a brazier's shop in Balokhati, while in the background craftsmen labor to make another one. A molten bar of brass is held with pincers by the brazier and beaten into shape with wedge-shaped mallets by his two sons.

Above: At a market in Ganjam District village potters sell their wares. Pottery vessels are used by poorer families for cooking and by all, except Brahmans, for storing water. Their shapes and decoration, as is the case with brassware, vary from area to area; these pots are characteristic of this region.

Left: Ikat *saris* are extremely sophisticated in Orissa and are valued throughout India. In a process similar to that used in Andhra Pradesh, the warps and wefts are tie-dyed before being woven. Although ikat weavings are produced in many Orissan villages, those made in Nuapatna in Cuttack District have some of the most intricate designs, as can be discerned from the warp threads shown here, in the process of being painted with starch to strengthen them prior to their placement on the loom.

Opposite: Orissa is justifiably famous for its cotton and silk textiles. While in most of India lack of patronage during the last century led to a marked decrease in the quality of weaving, textiles in Orissa actually improved. In this photograph a girl in Cuttack District spins cotton thread, using her toe to keep the thread taut.

Stone devotional images, such as those blending into the gnarled roots of this pipal tree, are to be found in villages all over India. They are ageless, some carved to represent gods, others simply left in their natural state, and have been worshiped for hundreds, if not thousands, of years. These, in a small village in Cuttack District, portray the deities Ganesha, Nandi, and Shri Devi, and have been dressed in cotton for daily *puja*, or worship.

Terracotta horses, known as *thakurani* in this state, are given to various gods and goddesses to protect the donor from inauspicious omens, to cure illness, or to guard the village. In Orissa, clay figures, such as these made by local potters and placed in an elaborately arched shrine dedicated to the goddess Mata Devi, are simpler in form but serve a similar purpose to those found in Tamil Nadu. (Puri District)

Once each year, in a custom common to many villages, the image of the principal deity of an area is placed in a carved and canopied palanquin and taken in festive procession to survey the territory under his protection and to visit the neighboring villages to receive their blessings. (Puri District)

Each Hindu home has its own shrine or specifically defined sacred spot. In very poor houses deities are often represented by inexpensive prints or the most elemental images. Icons of personal gods are more elaborate in wealthier households. This small wooden Vaishnavite shrine in a Brahman home in Balikhondalo, Puri District, is dedicated to Krishna, an incarnation of Vishnu, the god of preservation and continuity, who is represented in his various forms in bronze at the back of the shrine. In the front, between hibiscus flowers given in *puja*, are *salagramas*, black fossilized ammonite shells worshiped as symbols of Vishnu, and a bottle and can holding sacred oil and vermilion.

Left: Wall paintings in Orissa are most commonly dedicated to Lakshmi, the goddess of home and fortune. Painted with coconut fibers by the farmer's eldest daughter on Thursdays, considered an auspicious day for Lakshmi, the designs on this wall portray common symbols of the goddess: a central lotus flanked by elephants and peacocks and bordered by two kadamba trees, all symbols of prosperity and fertility. (Balikhondalo, Puri District)

Below: In the village of Dhunlo, Puri District, paintings are colored using local materials: burnt coconut shells for black and crushed brick for red—both added to a lime-washed base. Beneath Lakshmi's symbols of elephants carrying lotuses are paintings of *kalashas*, the vessels containing coconuts (here represented by stylized black ovals at the rim of the pots) and ashoka tree leaves; this design symbolizes fecundity, prosperity, and welcome throughout India.

Opposite: Doors in Orissa, as elsewhere in India, are decorated to beautify the home as well as to protect it from malevolent spirits. As this farmer's family is too poor to afford a carved door, the mother has painted her door with auspicious designs to honor Lakshmi during the Shankaranti Dakhira festival in January. (Dhunlo, Puri District)

165

Most Indian tribes live in remote areas that are difficult to reach. The dense, fertile jungle of Koraput District in southeastern Orissa is the homeland of numerous Adivasi (tribal) peoples. Almost every aspect of the forest is used by the Adivasis: hardwoods and bamboo for houses and tools; fruits and tubers for food; bark fiber for clothing, ornaments, ropes, and baskets; gourds for vessels and instruments. Even tribal gods are represented by simple wooden stakes.

TRIBAL ORISSA

India contains more tribal people—fifty-three million, accounting for seven percent of the country's total population—than does any other country in the world. The term "tribe" in India is used to signify preindustrial peoples, who are also frequently referred to as "primitive" or "aboriginal." They generally live in remote areas, have similar language and kinship systems as well as a general lack of social stratification, and are totemistic and usually animistic (as opposed to Hindu) in their beliefs. Hundreds of tribes, collectively called Adivasis, meaning "original inhabitants" (a clear implication of their pre-Aryan origins) live in the subcontinent. Adivasis differ from tribesmen in most other countries in that they are consciously, rather than circumstantially, isolated. They have been aware of each of the many cultural infiltrations into their regions, and, indeed, some have been assimilated by those cultures, but the rest have chosen to retain their unique societies and customs in close proximity to the greater Hindu society.

Orissa has the second-largest tribal population of any state. Most of its tribesmen, over one and a half million, live in Koraput District, a finger of land in southern Orissa that is wedged between Andhra Pradesh and Madhya Pradesh. A look at Koraput District will provide an ideal introduction to Indian tribal culture generally. It is Orissa's biggest district, one of the largest in India (almost exactly the same size as Maryland). It contains no cities and only ten towns, where government administrators and many of the district's Hindu minority live. Seventy percent of Koraput District is forest and its several high plateaus are bordered and divided by mountains. Two princely states, Jeypore (not to be confused with Jaipur) and Kashipur, maintained joint jurisdiction over the area in recent history, but as of independence, both were disbanded and incorporated into the new state of Orissa. Sixty-two distinct classified tribes speaking a total of thirteen major tribal languages occupy this district. Oriya is the language of administration and of the early Hindu settlements. Recent immigrations of farmers from Andhra Pradesh and Madhya Pradesh have also introduced the languages of Telugu, Marathi, and Hindi, but few tribesmen speak any language but their own.

Most tribes are divided into totemistic clans, each named after a particular animal, place, or object regarded as sacred. Marriage is usually exogamous; that is, prohibited within one's own paternal clan. In general, Adivasi women have much more freedom than women elsewhere in India. Society permits open social exchange between the sexes, and women work, eat, dance, and sing alongside men. Many tribes condone premarital sex, and adolescent affairs in no way impinge upon future marital plans. Tribes are intensely communal and cooperative; to show concern and to take responsibility for other tribal members is considered of paramount importance. Children partake of almost all activities and accompany adults everywhere. They are regarded as mature beings at an early age and learn, through example and practice, to accept responsibility. Although the basic rights of tribal communities are protected by the central government, they are politically autonomous as far as their own internal

Opposite, above: Most tribal houses, such as the Kuttiya Kondh dwelling shown here, have bamboo-supported thatched roofs and walls of wooden beams plastered over with mud. The exteriors of these walls are incised with geometric designs, traced by finger when the mud is still wet and then burnished to make them shine. (Ambodola, Koraput District)

Opposite, below: Orissan tribes vary in terms of both their relative isolation and the degree to which they have assimilated Hindu cultural practices. The Kuttiya Kondh are strong in Orissan politics and have much more commerce with the outside world than do the Dongaria Kondh. A clay planter for *tulasi,* an Indian species of basil that is sacred to Vishnu and used in daily Hindu worship, stands in front of a Kuttiya Kondh house in Batkul, Baudh Khondmals District.

Left: Indian tribal peoples are insular by choice and usually do not like to leave their own territories. Markets provide them with their only access to the outside world. Once a week, villagers carry vegetables, fruits, tubers, tobacco, and handmade ropes and baskets as much as fifteen miles to market, where they sell them as quickly as possible in order to be able to spend a couple of hours bartering for goods and enjoying the festive crowd. (Semiliguda, Koraput District)

Below, left: Hindu traders come from larger towns to supply tribal markets with provisions. Among the goods laid out for sale under this awning are rows of glass beads and bangles, small mirrors, tins of unguents and simple remedies, scissors, thread, small wooden banks, metal and plastic pots, and commercial foods.

Below, right: A Kuttiya Kondh shaman sells his services and cures at a village market in Baudh Khondmals District. In front of him, out of view, are herbal leaves and twigs, tins and bottles of potions, bear claws, eagle feathers—all of which are used in conjunction with incantations and special rituals aimed at healing physical and emotional ailments. In tribal religions priests and shamans (as opposed to temples and icons are the source of direct contact with the gods and also serve as interpreters of the deities' intentions.

A line of barbers belonging to the Bhandari caste give weekly shaves using straight razors and no soap or water. Barbers everywhere in India are trained in massage and simple healing. They also often double as priests for non-Brahman shrines. (near Jeypore, Koraput District)

The Bondo live in the mountainous region bordering the Machkund River in southeastern Koraput District. Part of a select group of tribes sprinkled throughout eastern and central India, they speak a pre-Dravidian language, clearly establishing their link to India's earliest inhabitants. According to religious proscription they must shave their heads and are not permitted to wear clothes. The women circumvent that law by wearing thin bands of cloth that do not quite meet in the back around their waists and masses of metal and glass necklaces; some have also recently started wearing shawls to the public market. The men wear the briefest possible loincloths. Women weave the cloth for their "skirts" themselves on backstrap looms, using bark fiber and cotton, and braid fine hay to make their headbands. (Mundiguda, Koraput District)

Bondo men believe that their women are the most beautiful in existence and all of the tribe's creative energy goes into their adornment. Bondos drink heavily and have violent tempers. Their unusual looks, dress, jewelry, language, and temperaments cause local Hindus to regard them as total savages and to belittle them. Here, a Bondo girl sells edible seeds in a market at Mundiguda, Koraput District.

Opposite, above: Young girls from the Paroja tribe often wear flowers in their hair and abundant jewelry. Rings made of Indian coins are popular, and noses and ears are pierced as a sign of beauty. Their colorful *saris* are supplied by nontribal traders known as Panos. (Pottangi, Koraput District)

Opposite, below: Paroja women, having finished their marketing at Mundiguda in Koraput District, rest in the shade of a tree and gossip with the women of other villages before starting their long walk home.

Above: A young Paroja girl shelters herself from the sun under an old umbrella while selling chilies and vegetables at a weekly market in Pottangi, Koraput District.

Center: Dance costumes resembling tigers and lions are sold on the street in Jeypore. They are made by Hindu craftsmen by stretching cloth and sculpting papier-mâché over a basket framework to which bamboo legs have been affixed, and are worn by stepping through the hole in the top and lifting the animal around the waist. Both Hindus and tribal peoples in costume partake in an annual spring parade dance called Kalaghodanata.

Below: Tribesmen arrive at markets in the late morning, sell and trade their produce to purchase tools, vessels, essential provisions, and occasional trinkets or jewelry, and generally leave by early afternoon to start the long treks back to their villages. (Malakangiri, Koraput District)

175

The Gadabas, like the Bondos, speak a pre-Dravidian language. They are cultivators and hunters who hire themselves out as porters to other tribes and to Hindus. The *sari* on the Gadaba girl at the left was purchased plain from traders and tie-dyed by its wearer. (Pottangi, Koraput District)

Traditionally the Gadabas spun and wove all their own cloth, but today, with mass-produced goods so readily available, fewer and fewer are practicing this ancient tribal craft. Here, an old, blind Gadaba woman spins cotton (which she received from a nontribal trader in exchange for grain) into thread outside her home. Her face was tattooed during adolescence to enhance her beauty. (near Semiliguda, Koraput District)

Using a mixture of the old woman's dyed cotton thread and a special plant fiber, her husband weaves a *kerong*, the cloth customarily worn by Gadaba women, on a backstrap loom. Two *kerongs* are worn, one around the waist and one like a shawl. Old tribal legends say that the first Gadabas wore tiger skins, and today's Gadabas attribute the striped designs of their own *kerongs* to an imitation of that pelt.

In the Jhodia village of Renga girls eligible for marriage traditionally attract suitors by forming a line, linking arms around each other's waists, and dancing and singing in high-pitched voices to the accompaniment of music played by the younger girls. The girls in this line are intently observed by the young men in the village.

Each tribe has its own tradition of music, song, and dance. Tribal poetry, usually set to music, is among India's most beautiful. Accompanied by simple two-stringed instruments young Kuttiya Kondh men in the village of Dongsurada, near Chandrapur, sing ballads recounting their finest hunts, the beauty of their mountains, and the loveliness of the girls they are trying to woo.

Although age is not closely recorded in tribal villages, this Kuttiya Kondh woman's grandson is a village elder and her great-grandson a mature man with a grown family. (She is said to be 114.) The Kuttiya Kondh still practiced human sacrifice when she was a small child. Through certain signs interpreted as gestures of the gods, sacrificial victims were specially appointed at birth. Considered sacred beings, they were greatly honored and spoiled until they reached maturity, at which time they were killed as offerings to ensure crop fertility. Human sacrifice was outlawed by the British in the nineteenth century, causing an Anglo-Kondh war that resulted in the death of thousands of Kuttiya Kondhs.

Ritual governs every aspect of a Kondh's life, from ceremonies dedicated to the soul of a child before birth to elaborate festivities at death. In Baudh Khondmals District, pubescent Kuttiya Kondh boys approach their village elders in prayer as part of a ceremony initiating them into manhood. The ritual demands that they prove their strength and agility in intricate dances and mock battles before the tribe will accept them as men.

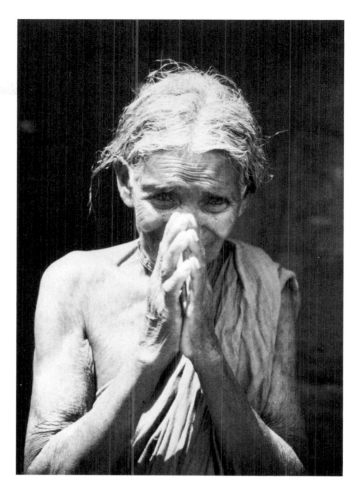

179

Opposite, above: As a preventive measure aimed at keeping tigers out of their homes, the edges of the thatched eaves on most Dongaria Kondh houses are purposely lowered to within only two to three feet of the ground. Inside, ceilings are surprisingly high and are surmounted by attics used for storing food, tools, and weapons. Houses usually have two or three rooms and no windows. The smoke on the hillside behind this village of Khajuri in Koraput District is the result of slash-and-burn cultivation, the farming method preferred by most tribes.

Opposite, below: Triangular designs made of turmeric and berry juice adorn the white lime-washed walls of the community meetinghouse, the center of village activity. As most tribes do not have temples per se, the meetinghouse often serves as a place for worship. Against the wall is an altar to Dhartanu, the Earth Goddess, most important of the Dongaria's numerous gods. The simple clay pots and wall paintings are symbols of devotion but, in contrast to Hindu temples, there are no icons here believed to contain the deity. Dhartanu's medium is the village priestess, or Bejjuni, who interprets for her while in a trance. (Khajuri, Koraput District)

Above: Against the outside wall of the meetinghouse are four carved dowels, each about a yard high, which serve as the villagers' only representations of their gods. Once every three years, during the Kandul Parba festival, a buffalo is sacrificed to Dhartanu, its flesh and blood buried at the corners of each cultivated plot to ensure continued fertility.

Right: The traditional costume of Dongaria Kondh women consists of two pieces of thick cotton cloth supplied by Hindu traders and then embroidered in bright designs by each woman. One is worn around the waist and the other draped to cover the breasts. Brass rings fashionably pierce the women's noses and upper ears, and numerous necklaces and other bangles are worn to further enhance their beauty. (Khajuri, Koraput District)

Opposite: Unlike Khajuri, the village of Kurli a few miles away has a mixed population of Dongaria and Panos (Harijan tradesmen-farmers, also known as Doms). The Panos serve as traders and servants to the Dongaria. The verandahs of Pano houses in Kurli are unique. Each one frames a wooden door intricately carved with designs that offset the bold geometries surrounding them. (Kurli, Koraput District)

Above: Pano houses in Kurli have common walls. The verandahs are separated by partitions of sculpted arches, columns, and niches, their sophisticated geometric shapes outlined in contrasting colors.

Right: The most striking feature of Pano verandahs is the way in which chairs, couches, and chaises are actually sculpted into them. Made of clay mixed with chaff, these pieces of "furniture" are plastered on a timber framework and painted with a colored slip, using burnt root for black, dark clay for red, and powdered chalk for white. The surfaces are then painstakingly burnished with a smooth stone until they shine. Their origin is a mystery, as these people are uneducated and have had little contact with broader civilization.

Village houses in West Bengal are often two stories and their thatched roofs generally have distinctive downward-curving eaves to facilitate the runoff of rain. Lower rooms are protected from the region's characteristically heavy rains by thatched awnings, which give houses the appearance of having two roofs. The lower awning of this home is in the process of being rethatched. (Daspur, Medinipur District)

Most of West Bengal is flat and intersected by countless rivers and streams that swell and flood during the usually heavy annual monsoon. Houses and roads are built, when possible, on high ground, while villages, like those of Kerala, tend to be loose conglomerates of widely dispersed farm dwellings or tiny hamlets, in which each house is oriented towards its own land. The level of literacy is high in West Bengal and most village children attend school. This group of uniformed schoolchildren are returning to their homes near Onda, in Bankura District.

WEST BENGAL

West Bengal is more familiar to Westerners than
any of the other states previously discussed. Its
capital city, Calcutta, is infamous. The deplorable
conditions existing there—the overpopulation,
poverty, and violence—have made that city a
textbook case for the media. Like any other major
city, it is not at all representative of its environs, but
is unique, and as such has little to do with a book on
rural India. The population of West Bengal is sixty-
one million. Three quarters of the state is rural and,
if Calcutta's population of ten million is considered
separately, the number increases to ninety-three
percent. Overpopulation and poverty afflict not only
Calcutta but many Bengali villages as well; the
causes and effects, however, are different.

In 1947 Bengal was split into two parts: West
Bengal became part of the Indian nation, and East
Bengal became first East Pakistan, and later, after
declaring itself independent, the new nation of
Bangladesh. Many of West Bengal's contemporary
difficulties stem directly from partition. Irrec-
oncilable religious differences between local Hindus
and Muslims led originally to the bifurcation of
Bengal, but in all other ways, in terms of geography,
heritage, language, and culture, the two areas are
homogeneous. Both halves of the original province of
Bengal are so similar, in fact, that many of the following statistics and descriptions of the state would
apply equally to its sister nation of Bangladesh. (The
term Bengal will be used to denote both areas. Also,
in describing the majority of West Bengal herein, two
smaller areas are neglected: the drier area to the

southwest, largely occupied by Adivasis, and the
thin band along the Himalayas, containing mountain
Hindus, hill tribes, and Tibetans.)

The nature of a people mirrors the nature of the
land they occupy. Bengalis are known for their
changeable passions, their intensity, their poetry,
their violence, and their arts; and the topography of
Bengal is one that changes constantly. Two major
rivers have created Bengal: the Ganges and the
Brahmaputra. Both cut through the Himalayas and
wind their way down through several other states
(the Ganges traveling from the west and the
Brahmaputra from the north) before reaching the Bay
of Bengal. Each river has brought with it the water
and silt from countless tributaries, thereby forming
one of the world's largest alluvial plains: Bengal.
More than a million tons of suspended matter is
carried into Bengal in this fashion every year, and
the topsoil is now thousands of feet thick and
incredibly fertile. Most of West Bengal is flat and
enmeshed with myriad rivers, streams, and canals,
which continually change shape and direction. The
land is perfect for producing such wetland crops as
rice, sugarcane, and jute, and much of the state
affords a semiannual crop, but the constant
alteration of currents and landmasses, when
combined with the violent extremes in weather,
makes crop yields undependable. Villagers
experience years of plenty alongside years of near
starvation. The prevalent worship in the area of Kali
and Durga, violent goddesses of creation and
destruction, gives expression to those extremes.

Villages have adapted to this terrain. Homesteads are so spread out, each clinging to a bit

185

Bamboo is the favorite building material in Bengal. It is light, strong, and pliable in heavy winds. The walls of this village house in Burdwan District are entirely woven of bamboo strips. Most houses keep wet bamboo and grass screens in front of their windows and doors during the summer to act as filters for the oppressive heat.

of high ground to avoid monsoon flooding, that villages, as is the case in Kerala, are usually defined according to individual loyalties and reflect a cohesive social order; rarely do they take the form of spatially defined clusters of dwellings. Houses are usually built near water for reasons of commerce and trade as well as for convenience' sake, but constantly shifting waterways have left many villages on high ground away from their original water source. Rooms in Bengali houses are not interconnected (each must be entered from the outside), and kitchens tend to be separate from the main dwelling; frequently different members of a joint family will live in clustered houses that share a kitchen. Walls are usually made of mud and support thatched, gabled roofs with drooping cornices. The houses of wealthy Bengalis are surrounded by verandahs and placed in the center of walled compounds (the word "bungalow" literally means "Bengali house").

When compared with that of other areas of India, Bengal's impact on history is relatively recent. The eighth until the thirteenth centuries saw periods of great development in learning and indigenous arts, first under the Buddhist kings, the Palas, and second under the Shaivite and Vaishnavite kings, the Senas. Five centuries of Muslim rule followed, during which time Buddhism was virtually wiped out and Islam gained countless Bengali converts. Muslim tolerance in the sixteenth century enabled a resurgence of Hindu culture, which manifested itself in the form of a powerful Vaish-navite Krishna cult, whose descendents still form a core of Bengal's rural religion. Europeans had been familiar with the name Bengal from the time of

Marco Polo. Bengal's position as a freshwater port linking the sea with the Gangetic Plain propelled the British to establish trading rights there in 1690. By 1765 Bengal had become the first true seat of administrative power for the British in India, and Calcutta remained their capital city until the twentieth century. Bengali silks as well as cotton muslins of the finest quality had long been prized in Europe, inspiring fashions from the Renaissance through the eighteenth century. The British initially capitalized on this trade, and rural Bengal prospered. By 1787 the Bengali production of textiles for foreign trade was valued at £625,000. Within a very few years, however, because of the Industrial Revolution, the agitation on the part of Englishmen for home production, and the resultant domestic manufacture of textiles in Britain, exports from India dropped drastically. By 1813 the export value of textiles was a meager £33,811, and large-scale Indian production had been shut down. The effect on the Bengali economy was staggering. Since that time there has been no major internal source of income in West Bengal other than agriculture, which, as already noted, varies tremendously from year to year. Severe overpopulation has further complicated the problem, making the income derived from agriculture insufficient to adequately support the population.

West Bengal has the second-highest population density in India (thirteen hundred people per square mile) and also the second-highest level of literacy (thirty-three percent above the national average). This indigenous interest in learning caused the Bengalis to be more receptive to English culture than most other Indians, and as a consequence English

standard schools, colleges, and universities were established throughout Bengal. One of the biggest problems today facing educated rural Bengalis, of which there are many, is overqualification. Most educated villagers want a job "in service," which means a salaried post, preferably in government, and there are far too few of these to go around.

The social system in West Bengal is not as stratified as it is elsewhere in India. Villages have fewer castes and class divisions, and prejudices are not as pronounced. Brahmans do not have as much power as they do in other regions. They are not indigenous to West Bengal and are treated as a minority. The most prominent high-caste land-owners are Kayasthas (scribes), but twentieth-century land redistribution has been so effective in Bengal that they no longer control much. The overwhelming majority of the population are farmers, who are viewed as relatively equal socially. The only operative social division revolves around land ownership; people are ranked according to land and wealth. Kinship systems are similar to those found in the rest of eastern and western India. Lineage is known and recorded for several generations back, and villagers must marry an unrelated person from another village. Among the higher castes there is a tendency for women to marry men of even higher social status. The extended family is the backbone of Bengali society. An unusual feature in the Bengali inheritance laws, called *dayabhaga*, permits the head of a family to give the ancestral property to whomever he deems worthy.

Opposite, above: Seven suits, each painted with the symbols of a particular god, make up the canvas deck of cards being used by these Bengali villagers for the traditional game of *ganjifa*, which has been played in India for centuries. Many Western games have their origins in India, among them chess, Parcheesi, and a variety of card games. As in the West, villagers gamble on the outcome of their cards, but most play for relatively low stakes.

Opposite, below: The farming season in Bengal is long and arduous. In Howrah District, near Calcutta, an exhausted farmer curls up next to his working partner to sleep.

The production of clay dolls and toys has a long history in Bengal. Archaeological excavations of sites over two thousand years old have yielded terracotta toys similar to those shown here, for sale in Birbhum District. Commonly used in festivals and in play, clay toys are made by over three thousand potter families in Bengal today.

Quilts (*kanthas*) are made of several layers of scrap cloth stitched together and embroidered by Bengali women to portray scenes from daily life—in this case, fishermen, fish, birds, and pinwheel-shaped suns. The finest, made by Tanti and Kayastha women, members of the weaving and scribe castes, have designs similar to those found in local floor and wall paintings—designs that have been carefully applied with running stitches to both sides of the quilts.

A clay planter for a *tulasi* bush is reminiscent of Bengali temple architecture. *Tulasi* leaves are integral to the daily worship of Vishnu, the god of preservation and continuity. Popular poetry praising Krishna, an incarnation of Vishnu, written by the Bengali poet Chaitanya in the sixteenth century emphasized the mystic adoration of the Universal Soul and restrengthened the Vaishnavite sect of Hinduism so prevalent in rural Bengal today. (Panchmura, Bankura District)

Faith and devotion are intense in rural Bengal, where conditions are difficult. Villages abound with shrines to local deities, each under constant worship to avert calamity and ensure a prosperous year. Garlands of flowers, sold on the roadside, are purchased by devotees for use in their daily worship.

One of the most pronounced qualities of village art is its immediacy. Much of it is created quickly of basic materials and is intended only for use in a specific ceremony, after which it is discarded. These tiny clay elephants and horses, many only inches high, have been given by village women to the shrine of Ma, the local Earth Goddess, as part of a vow (vrata) in return for special favors such as cures for illness or barrenness. (Bankura District)

Until very recently there were no bridges crossing the wide Ganges River anywhere in Bihar; it had to be crossed by boat. The river, running from west to east through the center of the state, thus effectively divided Bihar into distinct cultural regions.

BIHAR

Bihar is a state of dichotomies, split by geography, peoples, and history. Twenty-six centuries ago it became the seat of India's first empire, a center of progressive thinking and enterprise. For over a thousand years it remained the nucleus of northern Indian civilization. Now, unfortunately, it is the site of some of the country's worst conditions: overpopulation, poverty, and violence.

Buddha lived and preached most of his life in rural Bihar. In the sixth century B.C., Pataliputra became the capital of the Magadhans and subsequently of the Mauryans and of other later great empires that promoted Buddhist culture, art, theater, and literature; founded universities; and encouraged open thought. After A.D. 600 Bihar lost its far-reaching power and its kingdoms became fragmented, but its newfound introspection gave impetus to the development of rural cultures and to the restrengthening of indigenous Hinduism. Invaders from Karnataka, in the eleventh century, founded a kingdom in North Bihar in which there evolved a unique synthesis of southern and northern Indian Hindu customs and thought. The Muslims, arriving in the twelfth century, annihilated most Buddhists, leveling their universities and institutions. The ruler Akbar made Bihar an integral part of the Mughal Empire in the sixteenth century, and the state remained vital during the British reign. The farms of North Bihar supplied the British with opium and indigo, the former used to secure Chinese trade rights and the latter a mainstay of Western and Eastern textile production.

Contemporary Bihar has a reputation for conservatism, for reluctance to change. There is not as much concern for modernization in this state as in most others and as a result it has less public transportation, less electricity, and fewer paved roads in rural areas. Most districts are stagnant economically. The only resource for the majority of North Biharis is rice cultivation, which is often insufficient to support the population of seventy-three million. The most widely spoken language is Bihari, a dialect of Hindi, and the literacy rate, at twenty-six percent, is the second-lowest in India (a fascinating occurrence given the high rate existing in its neighboring state, West Bengal).

North Bihar is flat and crisscrossed with rivers, bounded by the foothills of the Himalayas and Nepal on the north and by the wide Ganges River on the south. Social mobility is restricted, and the most prominent castes are Goalas (previously cow and goat herders, now mostly farmers), Brahmans, and Kayasthas (scribes). Dissatisfaction with economic and social conditions has engendered violence throughout North Bihar. Organized crime, in the form of bands of thieves and highwaymen, is rampant, and radical political insurrections occur periodically.

South Bihar is primarily a hilly plateau covered with dense forest. Historically it has been relatively inaccessible to invaders and has thus provided ideal living conditions for the tribes residing there. Bihar has India's third-highest tribal population (six and a half million), most of whom live in the Chota Nagpur and Santal Parganas areas of South Bihar. Chota Nagpur also contains the nation's largest

supply of coal, its biggest iron and steel plant (at Jamshedpur), and is the site for a huge government project (the size of which is comparable to that directed by the Tennessee Valley Authority), on the Damodar River, where a series of dams has been constructed to aid in flood control and irrigation and to generate hydroelectric power. The revenue and other benefits derived from this massive system have altered the national and local economies but have done little to improve the overall state economy. They have, however, restructured the lives of local Adivasis (tribesmen), whose original cultures were somewhat similar to those of Orissa's tribesmen. Many Adivasis work in the industrial projects, sometimes occupying positions of higher authority than those of high-caste Hindus, and this situation is fundamentally altering the traditional social order. Tribesmen working on these projects usually live in company housing or in clusters of buildings on the outskirts of towns but remain in close contact with their ancestral villages. The trend towards the encroaching Hinduization of these tribes has been halted. The central government has a tolerant and protective attitude concerning most tribesmen in India, and the formation of tribal unions and cooperative societies in South Bihar has encouraged a resurgence of pride in traditional customs and lore. Tribal poetry, drama, dancing, and art have gained a new respectability, and, reassured, Adivasis are returning to traditions such as eating beef, a practice which is considered socially abhorrent by Hindus.

Creativity often burgeons when conditions are bleak. Despite, or perhaps because of, their many hardships, Bihari villagers have produced some of India's finest folk art. Designs and techniques inherited from ancient craft guilds are evident in contemporary paintings, bronzes, terracottas, jewelry, and textiles. Village art seems timeless, a tangible reminder of the direct link existing between the craftsman and the traditions and customs of his ancestors. Village artists use the most easily available materials, and techniques are devised to suit those materials. Images tend to be symbolic rather than representational, with proportions and contours exaggerated to convey the essence of the subject. As the majority of folk art is created for social or religious rituals, each piece is imbued with the particular spirit of the ritual for which it is intended and, in turn, conveys the exuberance and vitality of Bihar's rich rural heritage.

The village women of North Bihar, particularly those in the Mithila region of Darbhanga District, are masters of the technique of wall painting. It was in this region that Sita, the heroine of the *Ramayana*, one of the primary Hindu epics, was born. Maithili villages fostered the initial growth of Sanskrit as well as the resultant developments in literature and drama, and they contain that unique blend of southern and northern traditions epitomized by their historical overlords, the Karnatas. Walls are painted in response to numerous rituals and vows, the most important of which involve thread-tying ceremonies, in which young high-caste boys are initiated into manhood, and weddings. For the latter the walls of a special room are covered with paintings of gods and goddesses, thereby forming a bridal chamber, or *kobar ghar,* where the

couple spends its first few nights and where the wife will give birth to their children. In the last two decades, the inherited techniques of wall painting have been successfully adapted to the medium of watercolor on paper by the women of these villages, creating a vital cottage industry and a major source of income for a previously impoverished people.

Opposite: Government buildings, such as this post office in Jitwarpur, Darbhanga District, are often the most substantial structures in a village. The postal system, established by the British, covers all of India, although letters may take weeks to reach villages inaccessible by road.

Above: There is no pattern to the layout of villages in North Bihar. They usually consist of several small hamlets, each containing a particular caste. The population's reluctance to modernize has resulted in most villages being without electricity or any modern machinery. (Jitwarpur, Darbhanga District)

Opposite: The architecture of this village temple to the god Vishnu, poised on the edge of a tank (reservoir) in Jitwarpur, Darbhanga District, is indicative of the region's former wealth. Before entering the temple, villagers descend to the tank to wash their feet and teeth and to gargle, as they should anywhere in India prior to setting foot in an orthodox shrine.

Above: A family travels to the weekly market by horse-drawn cart.

Right: At Madhubani in Darbhanga District a *sadhu,* or Hindu religious ascetic, dressed up as Shiva, blesses shopkeepers and marketgoers in return for alms. The accoutrements of his costume—the ash, leopard skin, wooden cobras (around his neck and on his head), sacred beads, and trident (*trisula*)—are all symbols of Shiva, the god of creation and destruction.

The walls of Bihari houses are decorated for numerous occasions. This painting of a bull and rider, located in a village near Sakri, Darbhanga District, was created for the Shivaratri festival held in the Hindu month spanning February and March and honors Shiva.

Girls are taught to paint at an early age, learning the distinguishing techniques of their family's style, so that when they are grown and move to their own homes, they can take this knowledge with them. Skills have been passed down from mothers to daughters in this way for hundreds of years. Seated in front of a painting dedicated to Hanuman, the messenger of the gods, a Harijan painter from Jitwarpur, Darbhanga District, decorates a pot to be used in a wedding.

Twice a year, in the Hindu month spanning October and November and in that which spans April and May, Bihari women make vows to Surya, the sun god, promising to perform certain arduous rituals in exchange for special favors, such as pregnancy for barren women or health for a sick child. A festival called Chhatra, lasting several days, is the culmination of these vows. In one of the many ceremonies common to Chhatra a family has gathered in their courtyard in Patna District to pray and sing songs to Surya in front of temporary shrines made of sugarcane stalks. Within each shrine is a terracotta elephant containing several small oil lamps, and all are surrounded by the family's offerings of rice and fruit.

The next day the women who made vows take their offerings of food, flowers, and terracotta elephants to the nearest major water source (in this case the banks of the Ganges River). Deep in prayer, they wade into the water and immerse their offerings, after which the devotee and food are considered blessed (the elephants are left submerged). Many of the vows require penances—some more severe than others—in exchange for favors granted. For example, to fulfill her part of a vow a woman whose child has recovered from cholera might have to crawl on her knees several miles from her house to the river as an act of humility.

After the food has been blessed, it is taken back and distributed among the family. In India food is rarely wasted. As no priest is required for the Chhatra festival, the devotee is free to keep the edible portion of her offering after it has been blessed. In Hindu temples a portion of it is left as a tithe for the priest, while the remainder is consumed by the family who, in eating it, are said to absorb the blessing into themselves.

When the vows are completed and the offerings blessed the families join the throng from several towns and villages in a festival of merriment on the river's edge. Musicians play, acrobats and magicians perform, boats filled to bursting with spectators sail along the shore, and all rejoice. Festivals throughout India encourage sharing in ancestral rituals and give villagers a sense of unity with other Hindus as well as providing entertainment and a well-earned release from hard work.

This house, seen here during the monsoon season, is typical of rural houses in eastern Uttar Pradesh. Most are two-story dwellings, built in stages to fit the family's needs and budget. The basic unit consists of a large single room subdivided by mat partitions, and a loft for storage. As the family expands, a second unit is added to form an L, a third to form a U, and the last completes the square, enclosing the courtyard. As the owners of this house are not yet able to afford a second permanent unit, they have temporarily attached a shed made of sticks, which doubles as a barn and a place where the men meet and drink tea. (Varanasi District)

UTTAR PRADESH

Uttar Pradesh is one of India's largest states, covering 76,000 square miles and having a population of 119 million. (For comparison, it is less than three-fourths the size of California, but has almost five times as many inhabitants.) It consists of a long strip of land, in which there are four basic geographic regions. The Kumaun to the north, a mountain and foothill region high in the Himalayas, supports a mixed Hindu and Buddhist population. Farther south is the Tarai, a strip of marshy jungle which has only recently become habitable due to the eradication of formerly prevalent malaria. The remainder and majority of the state is divided into two large areas, both of which have enormous Hindu and fairly large Muslim populations: the east, which is a continuation of the fertile "wet crop" terrain found in Bihar; and the west, a much drier, rocky plain suitable for wheat cultivation. Most of the western plain is bounded by two rivers sacred to Hindus, the Ganges and the Yamuna, and the wedge of land thus formed is called the Doab. Like North Bihar, Uttar Pradesh was one of the areas in which Indo-Aryan civilization flourished and out of which grew some of India's most prominent kingdoms, empires, and cultural developments. The cities of this state remain as testaments to former glories: Mathura, where Krishna was born, and Brindaban, where he revealed his powers; Varanasi (also known as Benares), the most sacred city of the Hindus, where it is believed that the gods are most accessible to devotees; Allahabad, a pilgrimage center at the confluence of the two holy rivers; Agra, one of the capitals of the Mughals, which is renowned for the Taj Mahal; and Lucknow, a center for Islamic nobility and a focal point of the anti-English demonstration The Mutiny.

The many peoples who came and settled in Uttar Pradesh brought with them their castes, customs, and lore. Villagers are aware of this complex heritage and view their social system as a composite of these overlapping cultures. Although each community has a distinct composition, villages are very interdependent in this densely populated state. As kinship and lineage laws are strict and villagers must marry outside their own families and communities, a strong network of marital connections has evolved among neighboring villages. For example, in one village studied by the social anthropologist Bernard Cohn, the 256 women residents of the community had come from 200 distinct villages within a 40 mile radius; of the 200 women who had been born there all had moved to other villages upon marriage. The result was an infrastructure of rural interaction spanning four hundred villages at the time the survey was conducted. Women regularly visit their ancestral villages with their children, and members of widely scattered families join together for festivals and important ritual functions. Kinship is of utmost importance to villagers: the more relatives one knows, the better. Through relatives one achieves outside contacts and hence opportunities for economic, social, and political improvement. Local power and prestige are largely based upon one's associations and kin, and model family behavior is considered of paramount importance. Villages also

There is no particular pattern to villages in Uttar Pradesh. They are usually composed of several clusters of buildings built close together to conserve space, each cluster containing one caste or mutually compatible castes. Every available space is planted to support the state's burgeoning population.

maintain contact with the outside world through commerce, the demands of employment, and religious pilgrimages.

Social stratification is complicated in Uttar Pradesh, where the average village is composed of twenty-five to thirty different castes and twenty-one percent of the population is Harijan. The change in the economy wrought by the steady replacement of many locally made products with mass-produced ones has altered the traditional order. In western Uttar Pradesh the close proximity to major cities and the attendant exposure to modern technology, education, and media have made many rural people question the status quo. Villagers, especially men, are beginning to doubt the immutability of their social order, their rituals, and even their gods. Women, less educated and less exposed to the media, remain the mainstay of traditional culture and continue to practice their hereditary customs. They are much more protected than their counterparts farther east or in the south. Under orthodox Hinduism, which has historically been particularly strong in Uttar Pradesh, the duty of a woman is to serve her husband, her "master." The six centuries of Muslim rule in the area have only compounded this attitude. Throughout the state, lower castes are attempting to better their standing by altering their habits and customs—everything from their hair-styles and gestures to their rituals and holidays—to fit the requirements of higher society. Ironically, while the upper castes are becoming more liberated and less bound by caste, ritual, and dogma, the lower castes, in trying to improve their status, are imitating the traditional characteristics of their

superiors. In doing so, they grow ever more conservative and dogmatic (for instance, as upper-caste women become more emancipated, lower-caste women become more sheltered).

Increasing overpopulation in Uttar Pradesh is causing a drain on village resources. Ninety percent of villagers live off the land, their farms generally located within their village's boundaries. Rural population has tripled in the last century, and although modern farming techniques, better irrigation, higher-yield grains, and chemical fertilizers have greatly improved the output from these lands, there is little room for expansion. The forests and pasturelands which surrounded most villages a hundred years ago are now almost all farms. Redistribution of lands in Uttar Pradesh has been extensive since independence in 1947, but control still rests largely in the hands of the high castes, particularly with the village headmen, or *nambardars,* who are empowered by the state to collect taxes. Although *nambardars* inherit their positions, they can only maintain them by establishing political and socioeconomic connections.

Exceptions to these statistics of overpopulation and land division are found in the Tarai and Kumaun regions of northern Uttar Pradesh. The Tarai, an area at the southern edge of the Himalayas, was previously so infested with malaria that it was virtually uninhabitable. Within the past few decades, however, pesticides and vaccines have effectively combated the problem, and as a result the land is being reclaimed, jungles leveled, crops planted, and the population is growing. The region is as yet a relatively untapped frontier, where there are new villages, new farmlands, and, consequently, a freer attitude towards traditional occupational restrictions. The rough terrain of the Kumaun has inhibited population growth, and hard work combined with a wise traditional ecology has produced a self-sufficient agrarian economy.

The common language of Uttar Pradesh is Hindi, India's most widely spoken language. Hindi is almost identical in speech to Urdu (exhibiting only minor dialectical differences); it has the same origin but a different script. Hindi, spoken by Hindus, is written in *devanagari,* the script of Sanskrit, while Urdu, spoken by Muslims, is written in an Arabic script. Together these two variations on the same theme form the fourth most widely spoken language in the world. Before independence, Urdu was much more pervasive in Uttar Pradesh than it is today, spoken as it was by the millions of Muslims who left the state for Pakistan. Now it is spoken mostly by urban Muslims. Hindi is one of the principal languages of government in India, rapidly replacing English in much of the east and the west. For villagers, the standard use of Hindi is reinforced through films. These films, mostly lavish musicals made in Bombay, can be seen by villagers at nearby towns or regional centers. They are a major source of contemporary rural change: by making villagers aware of other peoples and customs and by challenging their beliefs and creating new mythologies, they are gradually introducing the values of modern Indian culture.

Left: The Himalayan Mountains in northern Uttar Pradesh rise abruptly from the Tarai, an area bordering the mountains' southern edge and lying at an altitude of one thousand feet. Most of the lower hills are terraced to support crops of rice, wheat, and vegetables. Fields are not irrigated, but regular rainfall and the systematic rotation of crops ensure consistent and adequate yields. (Tehri-Garhwal District)

Above: The ideal location for mountain villages is below the snow line at six thousand feet, and many cling to the hillsides at that altitude, their dwellings forming tight clusters. The customs and social mores of the majority of Paharis (mountain Hindus) deviate from those of lowland Hindus. For example, Paharis consult shamans, sacrifice animals, drink alcohol, permit widows to remarry, are sexually more permissive, and sometimes intermarry with other castes. (Kimoi, Dehra Dun District)

An intricately carved wooden pillared verandah runs the length of this home's second floor. Behind the verandah in most Pahari houses are isolated, closed rooms on either side, and in the center, interconnecting rooms, which usually contain two hearths for cooking and windows that are barred. Pahari houses are well adapted to the climate, blending wood and stone into a unique form of architecture. (Almas, Dehra Dun District)

Most Pahari houses are two stories: the living quarters are located above (reachable only from the outside via stone stairways) and the barns below. Narrow walkways run the length of the second story, often joining together separate houses. All rooms are entered from the front; the backs of houses are entirely closed. (Almas, Dehra Dun District)

Hundreds of thousands of villagers make the difficult pilgrimage every year to the mountain source of the Ganges. At one of the sacred spots (Hardwar) near there, pilgrims can purchase "leafboats" of marigold garlands, which, in dedication to the god Shiva, they float upon the river.

Above: Houses in eastern Uttar Pradesh, unlike those in the north, tend to be made of rammed earth built layer upon layer with no wooden supports. Roofs are supported by two layers of beams interspersed with flat boards that distribute the weight and are tiled with locally fired semicylinders.

Left: Having just made the small cooking stove in the foreground, these farmers' wives in Lohaipur, Deoria District, set to work on a huge vessel for storing rice. The stove is typical of eastern India: burning coals, usually made of dried cow dung mixed with straw, are tended inside, while round-bottomed cooking pots rest on the rings at the top. To make the storage vessel, slabs of clay are smoothed and joined together to form a ring, which is gradually built up to create a pot over six feet high.

Opposite: Many houses in Uttar Pradesh are built of bricks that are locally fired in huge kilns. Centuries of defense against invasion are apparent in rural village composition. Streets zigzag, no windows face the street, and entrances to houses are offset to inhibit passersby from seeing into inner courtyards. (Lohaipur, Deoria District)

Throughout India houses are cleaned and repainted for Divali, a festival in October honoring Lakshmi, the goddess of the home and prosperity. On Divali, the night of the new moon, each home is bedecked with hundreds of tiny clay oil lamps to glorify the goddess. As part of that ceremony elephants and riders have been painted by a farmer's wife on the walls of this inner courtyard in Bistauli, Gorakhpur District.

Elephants made to honor Mataji, the Mother Goddess, stand in a shrine in Gorahwa, Gorakhpur District. Terracottas of more "refined" shapes are mass-produced in villages not ten miles away and sent to handicraft emporiums all over India. Potters, such as those who made these sculptures, are anonymous and retain the essence of unselfconscious creativity.

Top: A rural potter's kiln in western Uttar Pradesh bears little resemblance to the Tamil one shown on page 116. This dome-shaped kiln is a permanent structure with clay walls and an opening at the back where smoke can escape. Cow dung, the area's primary source of fuel, is here being formed into bricks.

Left: A Muslim weaver's wife in Tanda, Faizabad District, has set up a spindle for spinning two-ply cotton thread on the street in front of her home. Historically the weavers of this area have produced some of the country's finest cotton muslins.

Above: The favorite entertainment of a local *mela*, or fair, is the Ferris wheel, a device invented in this part of the world and still propelled by the most traditional of means—human strength.

213

Left: Festivals bring villagers to the many towns and cities in Uttar Pradesh. A family of farmers has come to Delhi in a cart drawn by this bullock, dressed in full regalia especially for the occasion.

Below: A *sadhu*, or Hindu religious ascetic, has "set up shop" at the edge of a village market in Saharanpur District. In return for alms, he gives mantras and talismans and promises to heal illnesses as well as to exorcise evil spirits.

Opposite, above: A priest dressed as Hanuman, the gods' messenger in monkey form, leaps and dances among a crowd gathered at a rural temple to honor an ancient guru in Saharanpur District.

Opposite, below: In an attempt to purify their souls, religious Hindu zealots on pilgrimage in Varanasi (Benares) have had their bodies completely tattooed with the Sanskrit words "Rama, Rama, Rama," one of the many names given to God.

THE WEST

This Rabari man (a member of a local caste of farmers and herdsmen in Kutch, Gujarat) wears the distinctive costume—the gold earrings, silver necklace, shawl, and embroidered tunic—of his particular village. Rabaris are primarily pastoral, their major income derived from the sale of milk and *ghee* (clarified butter), but some nonetheless raise subsidiary crops. Although they do not weave, Rabari men spin yarn as they tend their flocks.

Forty percent of India's total landmass is contained in its four western states: Madhya Pradesh, Maharashtra, Gujarat, and Rajasthan. In three directions the region's boundaries conform to natural divisions: in the south a change from red to black soil distinguishes its Deccan region from that of Andhra Pradesh's; in the north plateaus, mountain ranges (the Aravalli and the Vindhya), and desert separate it from Uttar Pradesh, Punjab, and Haryana; and in the west almost impenetrable deserts (the Rann of Kutch and the Thar) divide it from Pakistan. Linguistic and political differences, rather than geographical ones, determine its eastern boundary, for the plateaus, plains, and mountains of Madhya Pradesh are unchanging extensions of those of South Bihar and Orissa. Deforestation is a serious problem, particularly in Rajasthan and Madhya Pradesh, where broad areas of trees are annually cut down by Hindu and tribal villagers in desperate need of cooking fuel. The government has tried to prevent this deforestation, but inadequate restrictions combined with rural ignorance concerning soil protection have resulted in much of this land becoming barren.

The overall population of western India is 204 million, or approximately 27 percent of the country's total. Of this number the highest concentration lives in the southern coastal region between Bombay and Ahmedabad. Post-independence migrations of Hindus and Muslims between the western states and Pakistan were extreme, and as a result enormous changes have been introduced into many traditional communities. Of the three major languages used in the region all have a Sanskritic base; Hindi is spoken in Rajasthan and Madhya Pradesh, and Gujarati and Marathi in Gujarat and Maharashtra respectively. The majority of India's tribesmen, over twenty-five million, live in western India, many of them speaking their own languages derived from Dravidian and Munda (a pre-Dravidian family of tribal languages) sources. The literacy rate and economy vary among the four states. Gujarat and Maharashtra are highly literate, progressive, and industrialized; Madhya Pradesh is underdeveloped and has a low level of education; and Rajasthan, one of India's least literate states, is impoverished but beginning to improve its economic outlook by implementing massive irrigation programs and by encouraging tourism.

There is no standard pattern for village layout in western India; each geographical and cultural area has its own style. A history of militancy in the region, however, of centuries of wars and battles, has resulted in the fortification of many villages. Communities are accordingly often comprised of tight clusters of buildings (whose windows and doors open inwards) surrounded by thick ramparts. The primary food staple of western India, unlike that of the south and most of the east, is wheat, generally eaten in the form of unleavened breads (*chapattis*, or *rotis*). Most villagers in Maharashtra and Gujarat are vegetarian, while those in Rajasthan and Madhya Pradesh are not. The most distinctive aspects of western Indian dress are the long turbans (*pagris*) worn by many men in the three northernmost states and the wide pleated skirts (*ghagras*) worn with blouses and long mantles (*odhanis*) by the women of Rajasthan and Gujarat.

Broad generalizations regarding these western peoples are impossible. The west includes India's most martial people, the Rajputs, and its most non-violent, the Jains; it contains highly sophisticated and worldly peoples, the Marathas near Bombay and the Gujaratis near Ahmedabad, for example, as well as very insular and "primitive" groups, such as some of the tribesmen of Madhya Pradesh. The economy is essentially controlled by four social groups: the Jains, Parsis, Marwaris, and Rajputs. The Jains, although they account for less than two percent of the western population, are disproportionately powerful. Basically atheistic and ascetic, they believe that each atom of creation—from plants, animals, and rocks to liquids and gases—has a soul. The soul is said to be entrapped in matter and defined by *karma,* and one's duty in life is to cleanse, and thereby release, one's soul from that entrapment. This can only be achieved by leading a pure life—through right faith, right knowledge, and right conduct, the latter requiring chastity, honesty, nonviolence, and unconcern for worldly things. Jains must choose between a monastic and a secular life. Since they may not farm, as harvesting involves killing plants, they primarily find employment in business careers, excelling as merchants in the rural and urban societies of western India. The Parsis are followers of the ancient Persian prophet Zoroaster, who promoted the worship of the sun god and sacred fire, and are descended from immigrants who were forced to flee from their native Persia when Islamic hordes invaded after the seventh century A.D. They are among India's wealthiest businessmen, but as they constitute an extremely small urban minority in Maharashtra and Gujarat, they stand outside the scope of this text. The Marwaris are a widespread mercantile class living in towns and villages throughout much of India. Their ancestors, who came from the bleakest part of India, the Thar Desert, where conditions can support only a sparse agricultural and pastoral population, turned to commerce and trade, funding caravans and encouraging the export of crafts. Today Marwaris are rural and urban bankers and moneylenders who control the economies and lives of many villages and villagers.

The Rajput class rose to prominence in response to the first Islamic invasions of western India in the eighth century. Their primary characteristics are martial chivalry and a tendency to assimilate a wide variety of castes. They gained ownership of most of the land in Rajasthan, Gujarat, and western Madhya Pradesh through strength, bravery, self-sacrifice, and ingenuity as well as through intermarriage with indigenous castes, which broadened their "membership." They legitimized their claims to rightful rulership by providing (questionable) genealogies linking their ancestry to the mythological Solar and Lunar races, and thereby succeeded in establishing literally hundreds of small kingdoms throughout the area. The Rajputs presented a formidable obstacle to the early Muslim sultanates of northern India but through mutual respect became invaluable allies of the Mughals. The British officially recognized the Rajputs' claim to their lands and for the first time in history fixed the boundaries of their kingdoms through treaties that allowed them to maintain traditional forms of administration but required allegiance. In modern India the millions of Rajputs

are the major landowners in the west, and their ideals of chivalry and leadership continue to inspire the gradual assimilation of less socially acceptable peoples into their ranks, among them many Hinduized tribesmen.

The Bhils are one such tribe who live mostly in the mountainous regions of all four states. Although historically they ranged throughout western India, most contemporary Bhil communities are located in isolated, relatively infertile areas, where farming is difficult and conditions are poor. While some of those living in the more remote villages have retained their traditional customs and lifestyles as migratory gatherers, hunters, fishermen, and herdsmen, most are now farmers who live in settled communities and accept Hindu beliefs, rituals, and notions of social order. Though many still speak their native tongue, Bhili, the majority have adopted the dialects of their home states. They still consider themselves tribal, and continue to worship their hereditary tribal gods (such as Gothriz Purvez) alongside the newly introduced Hindu gods (the principal deities of which they refer to simply as Bhagwan).

As was stated in the Preface, this book focuses upon those areas in which the author has conducted field research. Maharashtra was not among them and consequently is not described or illustrated in detail. As it is, however, an integral part of western India, it is herein accorded a brief mention. Maharashtra is a large state, roughly 123,000 square miles, and is bounded by Gujarat, Madhya Pradesh, and Karnataka. Contemporary cultural mores and innovations radiate out from Bombay, India's greatest port. Maharashtra's population of seventy million provides more gross industrial output than does any other state, and its Socialist government has instigated massive agrarian reform. Its largest rural caste is comprised of Marathas, descendents of the rulers of a powerful empire which rose in the seventeenth century to combat Mughal aggression. Under the brilliant military leadership of a man named Shivaji, the Maratha martial clans spread as far as Bengal and Punjab and are still influential in Madhya Pradesh. Shivaji has become a cult figure throughout Maharashtra and is revered in the temples of many villages as a semideity. The lives of nearly five million Mahars, a Harijan subcaste, have been altered in Maharashtra as a result of a rather unusual occurrence—all have converted from Hinduism to Buddhism. Originally, the Mahars were village servants—sweepers, guards, and messengers—who came to national attention when Gandhi focused upon them in his appeals for social revolution. Their leader, Dr. Ambedkar, became the minister of law in independent India's first Cabinet and thirty years ago began a successful campaign to convert the Mahars to Buddhism. Prior to his campaign there were less than two hundred thousand Buddhists left in the subcontinent; today there are millions, most of them Mahars, farming in villages all over Maharashtra and in southern Madhya Pradesh. Though they still must struggle to survive, the Mahars' new casteless identity has given them self-respect and the resolve to further better their position, which is gradually improving.

The rugged terrain of Madhya Pradesh proved an effective barrier to invasion in earlier times. India's largest state, Madhya Pradesh still has vast tracts of unexplored jungle that contain the subcontinent's largest tribal population. As far as the eye can see from this promontory at Tamia in Chhindwara District, no roads or large communities dot the landscape.

MADHYA PRADESH

Madhya Pradesh is India's largest state, covering most of central India and including the territory known during the British administration as the Central Provinces. Its vast, almost impenetrable forests, mountain ranges, steep plateaus, and deep river gorges and canyons comprised the major stumbling blocks to any incursions from the north into the south. The dense jungles, forbidding to any army, gave sanctuary to India's largest and most diverse tribal populations. It was to this area as well as to the plateaus of South Bihar and the mountains of western Orissa that these tribesmen's ancestors came when they were pushed out of the Gangetic Plain by the early Aryans. The state contains two major mountain ranges, the Vindhya and the Satpura, and two major rivers, the Narmada and the Tapti. The valleys created by these two rivers and the dry, scrub forest areas of the Malwa Plateau in northwestern Madhya Pradesh were primary sites of early Hindu settlement. Great Hindu kingdoms flourished here until the seventeenth century, when they were supplanted by the Mughals. As the general population of the subcontinent has inflated within the past two centuries, and as more modern methods of transportation have made the area increasingly accessible, Madhya Pradesh has become an area of Hindu colonization and settlement. Many of its villages and towns today have a frontier quality. The state's major crops are wheat, millets, and cotton in the west and rice in the east, and the whole state is the source of India's finest supply of teak wood, which is in demand all over the country. In addition to its wealth in agriculture and forestry Madhya Pradesh contains some of the country's most important and as yet untapped mineral and fuel reserves in its previously inaccessible plateaus and mountains, making it a significant area for future development and an economic boon to the country as a whole.

Because of Madhya Pradesh's inaccessibility and the ruggednesss of its terrain, the population in this state is lower than that of most other states. For example, although it is more than five times as big as West Bengal, its population of fifty-eight million is less than that state's. Compared to the rest of the country, its railway lines and good roads are few, and industry is underdeveloped. Madhya Pradesh has no cultural or geographical epicenter; its varied population is dispersed throughout the region. Descendents from the ancient kingdoms live in the broad river valleys and cultivated plateaus interspersed with more recent settlers from the neighboring states of Maharashtra, Gujarat, Rajasthan, Uttar Pradesh, Bihar, West Bengal, and Orissa. Hindi is the most widely spoken language in the state, although immigrants from peripheral cultures have brought their dialects with them, and tribal languages are spoken in isolated pockets. Traditionally banditry was considered an acceptable way of making a living by many of the region's castes and some tribes (labeled "criminal castes" by the British), and although, over the past century, severe punishment has been meted out to these bandits or *dacoits,* and attempts at their rehabilitation have been made, changing the customs of most of them, there are still many

221

throughout the state, and travel at nighttime is dangerous.

Almost twelve million tribesmen live in Madhya Pradesh, all of them belonging to one of two categories: those who have retained their hereditary culture and social order, and those who have become Hinduized, adopting the settlement patterns, dress, and many of the socioreligious customs of the neighboring Hindu farmers. Aside from these tribes there is a large population of Harijans, most of whom are descended from the tribal converts of previous generations. Together these Harijans and tribesmen account for one third of the state's total population.

The largest of Madhya Pradesh's many tribes is the Gonds, whose members number nearly six million if the subsidiary branches in Maharashtra, Orissa, and Andhra Pradesh are included. While most Indian tribes have remained insular by choice, the Gonds, a Dravidian people, are unusual in that they ruled a powerful and well-organized kingdom in central India for several centuries and were socially recognized by their Hindu peers. They were conquered and disbanded in the eighteenth century by the Marathas and today are scattered thoughout their previous kingdom. Within the last fifty years, the amount of land owned by the Gonds has decreased markedly because of the superior commercial ingenuity of immigrant Hindu farmers and moneylenders, who loaned the Gonds money, charging exorbitantly high interest rates, called in their loans, and then claimed the Gonds' land as payment. Most Gonds now live in Bastar District (bordering Koraput District in Orissa), located at the southeastern tip of the state, where they and neighboring tribes have been the focus of ongoing anthropological studies. Largely because of the work of these researchers and of social workers, the state and central governments are now aiding and protecting the rights of Madhya Pradesh's tribes, whose communities are situated in what are offically designated as protected forests. The Gonds' social order is remarkably egalitarian, exhibiting little hierarchy or class distinction. Kinship systems follow a Dravidian pattern, in which the maternal first cousin is considered the most desirable mate. Marriage, although it may be encouraged or arranged by the family, is generally based upon agreements reached by a couple in late adolescence or adulthood, and the ceremony is simple. Sexual attitudes are tolerant, and divorce and remarriage frequent.

Rules governing betrothal, marriage, and kinship among Madhya Pradesh's Hindus are similar to those existing for most eastern and western Indians. An exception involves exogamy (marriage outside one's village), which is preferred but not required. Even though the minimum legal age for matrimony was set at fifteen in 1955 and raised to sixteen a few years later, marriage among children is still common. Few children, except those from the lowest castes, would consider the possibility of choosing their own spouses. It is the responsibility of the girl's father to arrange the betrothal, and an important consideration for the groom's family involves the amount of dowry (although technically illegal in modern India) that the girl will bring with her. Marriage in rural Madhya Pradesh, as else-where in India, is the concern of the whole village. A

family hopes to improve its financial and social status through marriage, and a village builds its reputation on the nature of the brides it produces and of those it receives. Villagers believe that it will be easier for a girl to adjust to the idea of living with her in-laws if she has been acquainted with them from an early age. Thus, a girl married in infancy or childhood, though she will live with her parents until she has reached puberty and they feel she is old enough to live with her husband, frequently meets with her future family and husband. Virginity, of primary concern to any strict Hindu, is an absolute condition of any prepubescent alliance. Only after the couple has reached puberty and the time is considered propitious may the marriage be consummated. Often the new couple will be unable to share a private room; they sleep separately, the girl with the women and the boy with the men and animals (other members of the household give them temporary privacy when they request it). It is considered improper for newlyweds to speak together in public, and only after several years, when they have produced at least one male child, is this restriction eased. In Madhya Pradesh a "pitcher ceremony" symbolizes a bride's welcome into her new family and community. She draws water from the village well and offers it to the household deities and to the family elders. In receiving drinks from her, family members are ritually accepting her into the family and making her a part of its lineage, a position which she will maintain throughout her lifetime and which will require her newfound family to honor her in death.

The village of Udayagiri—a shapeless cluster of houses located close to a water source—is typical of village composition in western Madhya Pradesh. Because of heavy deforestation and only one season of rain a single annual crop of wheat and cotton is all that is produced here.

Villages in the eastern part of the state have a linear orientation, similar to that found in Orissa. Houses are generally made of mud surmounted by curved tile roofs. Here, brown geometric patterns have been added to whitewashed walls to beautify the street of a village where low-caste farmers live. (near Chabi, Mandla District)

Women of the Gond tribe, the largest in Madhya Pradesh, adorn the walls of their homes in Mandla District with secular decorations in bas-relief, using thick clay mixed with chaff. Designs vary from house to house, and women whose work is considered particularly fine are held in high regard.

Opposite, above: Carts vary throughout India. The roof of this farmer's bullock cart is made entirely of bamboo basketry. (Hoshangabad District)

Opposite, below: In Jabalpur District bullock carts are low-slung like sulkies and afford rapid movement. These bullocks' backs have been covered with brightly appliquéd cloths for market day.

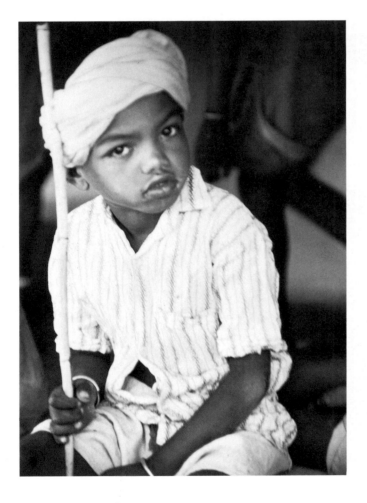

The Gonds can be divided into two basic groups: those who have resisted change, speak their original Dravidian dialect of Gondi, and call themselves Koitur; and those who have been assimilated by the broader Hindu culture, speak Hindi, and call themselves Gonds. The clothes of a Gond boy from Tamia in Chhindwara District indicate the blending of two cultures; he wears a traditional turban and a Western-style shirt.

The Korkus, a smaller tribe living in southern Madhya Pradesh, believe that the spirits of their dead will haunt them and cause misfortune and illness if not placated. To mollify them wooden tablets are carved naming and depicting them in positions of honor, usually on horseback, and all of the tablets for each village are placed together under a sacred tree. (Pachmarhi, Chhindwara District)

Low-caste village women from Raisen District wear their dowry
in the form of heavy silver and pot metal bangles, armbands,
and anklets.

A Harijan woman from Sehore District sits in the courtyard of her home after a hard day's work in the fields. The position of women in contemporary rural communities is changing. Societal pressures are still brought to bear, encouraging subservience, but because of the many recent female public figures in India who have contradicted the stereotype, many village women are now beginning to reexamine their roles.

A Baniya (merchant) sells raw sugar called *jagri* in a market in Raisen District.

This tribal market in Hoshangabad District differs from those of
Orissa in the large number of cattle present. Although they often
take poor care of their stock, most tribes in Madhya Pradesh
raise cattle to use in cultivation and sometimes to eat.

A Muslim villager buys a cooking pot in Seoni District. These pots have been thrown on a wheel and are paper-thin. The black pottery is fired separately from the red, its color achieved by sealing the kiln and reducing the available oxygen.

Northern Gujarat merges with Rajasthan to form a vast arid plain capable of supporting only subsistence farming. Farther south the alluvial deposits of several rivers make the state's Saurashtran peninsula perfect for growing lucrative cash crops, among them some of India's finest cotton.

GUJARAT

From the time of India's first settlements, Gujarat has been an area of shifting populations. Its long coastline and numerous harbors have made it a focus of maritime travel and trade. Its first communities, appearing contemporaneously with the Indus Valley Civilization in about 2500 B.C., were built as ports, and the world's earliest Asian and Western literature refers to the value of Gujarat's trade goods. Buddhists and Jains ruled there until the end of the eighth century. The former were eventually eradicated after a thousand years, but the latter still comprise a small part of the population and exert strong economic and political influence. The peaceful, nonviolent cultures of both these groups gave way during India's Middle Ages (extending roughly from 700 to 1200) to the militaristic feudalism of Hindu Rajputs. By assimilating the local middle classes the Rajputs strengthened their land base and to this day they still control most rural Gujarati farmlands. The western portion of Gujarat provided the early Muslims with their primary entryway into the subcontinent, and for several centuries most of the present state was under Muslim and Mughal rule. With the expansion of the British Empire, mainland Gujarat, under the jurisdiction of the province of Bombay, was directly governed by the British, while Saurashtra and Kutch, the current state's central and northwestern portions, respectively, were divided into 202 princely Rajput states.

Contemporary Gujarat is one of India's most progressive states. Mahatma Gandhi was born and raised here and he believed that his affinity for pacifism and social reform was an inherent Gujarati trait. The former capital, Ahmedabad, was host to his early career of political and social activism. Gujaratis are known for their resourcefulness and their business acumen and have successfully emigrated and thrived in communities around the world. (The majority of Indians in England, the United States, and Africa are Gujaratis.) Historically this area has been famous for its textile production (silks, embroideries, calicos, and chintzes), and its factories and rural handlooms produce more cloth than does any other state, giving it a large export revenue.

Social and cultural reforms since independence have been enormous in Gujarat. This state has the fourth-highest literacy rate in India (forty-four percent); most young adults can read; and newspapers, books, and magazines in the native language, Gujarati, are increasingly popular. The state is roughly the same size as Karnataka and has a slightly smaller population (thirty-eight million). Due to heavy industrialization, twenty-eight percent of Gujarat is urban. The espousal of anticaste attitudes by Buddhists, Jains, and, most recently, by the followers of Gandhi has helped to bring about a large middle class and a reduction in the number of Harijans (only 6.6 percent of the population), who, while still poor, are no longer treated as pariahs. Most of the state's five million tribesmen live in the east and are akin to those living in the bordering regions of Madhya Pradesh and Rajasthan. Gujarat is bounded by sea, by mountains, and by desert and is divisible into three distinct geographical sections: a

233

Villages on the Gujarat-Rajasthan border are compact, the houses huddled together to form defensive units. Crops of oilseeds are planted in small plots delineated by the remains of rock walls. (near Abu, Sirohi District)

portion in mainland India to the east, a large peninsula of land in the center called Saurashtra, and an isolated, arid strip to the west called Kutch.

Saurashtra, formerly known as Kathiawar, is a fertile alluvial plain; its black soil is rocky and sandy but ideal for growing crops of cotton, peanuts, oilseeds, and millets. Agriculture, as elsewhere, forms the backbone of village economy, but in this area the redivision of lands and the pooling of labor have provided a successful agrarian commerce founded on the cooperative use of small farms and advanced technology. (Modern machines such as tractors are increasingly popular cooperative purchases.) Because of the aggression of their Rajput and Muslim overlords most villages were built as defensive units, and today many still surround hill fortresses. Houses stand close together, facing inwards, and have highly fortified outer walls. Side streets end in culs-de-sac, called *pols,* which are the focal point of activity for extended families, clans, or subcastes. Farmlands are traditionally situated outside the village compound, and each plot is walled in stone, containing a small hut in which the owner or his son stands guard at night. Even today villagers bring all their livestock into the fortified village at night, according to age-old habit, although contemporary political stability has enabled villages to expand beyond their former walls, and rural peripheries are sprinkled with small farms.

Kutch, located directly on the Tropic of Cancer, is a sandy, treeless plain bounded by sea and desert. Its annual rainfall is less than ten inches, yet much of it is flooded each year during and after the monsoon by cumulative runoff from the rivers and

streams of northern India and Pakistan. Villages built on high ground in its northern sector literally become islands for months, and because of this extreme isolation unique local customs have evolved. Kutch's major cash crop is cotton, grown in the south; in the north and east most communities are pastoral, subsisting by raising cattle, buffalo, sheep, goats, and camels and selling milk and milk by-products. Men tend the flocks during the day, and during times of drought must look for fodder, which sometimes requires that they be absent from their families for weeks at a time. Women stay at home, caring for the children, churning and preparing milk, and, in their spare time, sewing and embroidering. Villages are spread out, tend to be less fortified than in Saurashtra, and are generally grouped according to caste or tribe. Kutch has a large population of Muslims, many of whom are herdsmen residing in the western Banni region. Although strict Sunni Muslims (the most orthodox Muslim sect), these clans are tolerant of their Harijan neighbors, and a unique blending of the customs, costumes, and settlement patterns of the two groups has arisen. The practice of *purdah* (in which women wear veils and are secluded) is rigorously observed by both groups, and in each a woman's life is centered around her home. Bannis are endogamous, meaning that they marry within their own village; the ideal arrangement is thought to be one in which the daughters from two close families are exchanged, with each marrying the other's brother.

Gujarati craftsmanship is unsurpassed. Historically the state's wealth was derived from its crafts, and a substantial proportion of its contemporary revenue is still generated in this way. Fine artistry is honored everywhere in Gujarat, and the ancient artisan guilds have lasted longer in this state than in any other. Although many crafts are factory-based, cottage industries are well organized and have rural cooperatives through which to market their products. A primary source of supplementary income for villagers in Kutch and parts of Saurashtra is textile production, particularly embroidery and appliqué. Originally made as part of each family's dowry for its daughters, these textiles have recently gained a wide Indian and foreign market.

Dowry is still important to Gujarati villagers (although here, too, it is technically outlawed). Both Hindu and Muslim women of many communities start sewing and embroidering years before a family wedding. The dowry is the bride's personal property; it is what she takes with her when she goes to her new home. It includes blouses, skirts, shawls, veils, quilts, covers, bags, and wall decorations, as well as jewelry and households goods—in short, everything she will need for the first few years of married life. Clothing receives most attention and is embroidered with the special designs and in a style that is unique to the maker's caste or community. So distinctive are these various decorations, in fact, that a Kutchi woman's village, caste, age, and status can be determined from her clothing. Through the items of her dowry a Gujarati girl establishes a link to her ancestry as well as to the rural traditions that define her place within the community.

The Rayisputra Maldharis (Muslim herdsmen) of Birandiala
village in Banni, western Kutch, live in round houses. These
houses have only one room, their walls are constructed of
covered-over sun-dried mud bricks, and their roofs consist of fans
of sticks tied to central pillars supported by crossbeams.
Separate rectangular huts comprise small kitchens and rooms for
entertaining visitors. In these, men smoke and talk.

Houses are regularly resurfaced with a mixture of mud and dung (*kaccha*), which is kneaded to a sticky consistency by the Banni women. This woman is wearing the local married Muslim woman's traditional dress of a printed, multipleated skirt, an embroidered blouse, a wide, printed veil called an *odhani*, and dowry bangles. (Birandiala, Banni, Kutch)

The mud and dung preparation is applied by hand to the walls, inside and out, and to the floors. After it dries, the walls are then whitewashed. This Maldhari woman wears a tie-dyed *(bandhani)* veil and a skirt painted with resist dyes. (Birandiala, Banni, Kutch)

The women of many villages in Saurashtra and Kutch make bas-reliefs in mud to adorn their interiors. The grain storage bin and dowry chest in this house, located in a Banni Muslim village, have been decorated in geometric designs and inset with mirrors. On top of the chest are tiers of brass pots, and to the side and front are several folded quilts, all part of the household dowry. (Hodka, Banni, Kutch)

Seated in her kitchen the wife of the village headman of Dhordha, Kutch, makes wheat *chapattis* for her family's dinner. Most Gujaratis are vegetarians; their food, famous for its subtle blend of herbs and spices in rich sauces, is among India's finest. A village woman might well spend hours in her kitchen each day preparing her family's meals.

The arms, feet, calves, neck, and chest of this Daysee Rabari woman (a member of the local caste of farmers and herdsmen in Mokhana, Kutch), have been tattooed as a sign of beauty. Wearing the standard dress of a middle-aged woman, she stands in front of her dowry chest, on top of which rests a stack of appliquéd quilts. Storage containers lining the shelves at the right hold spices used in daily food preparation.

Top: The principal room in the house of a Rajput landowner from Athkot, Saurashtra, displays his relative affluence. A Western-style oil portrait is flanked by two prints of gods and Victorian corner cabinets appear on either side of the room.

Left: A Dhed (weaver) from Bujodi, Kutch, prepares a woolen *dhabla*, or shawl, on a pit loom. The geometric border patterns are dictated by the customer, but each caste or village area usually has its own traditional preferences.

Above: Rathva (tribal) potters of Chota Udaipur in Baroda District throw large clay vessels on their wheels and then shape them into sculptures of tigers, elephants, and horses, which are placed in shrines to propitiate the restless souls of ancestors.

240

Kathi women, the wives of landowning farmers, from Saurashtra carry brass water pots from the village well. Beaded rings are placed on the top of their heads to support the pots.

An old Jain pilgrim is carried on a palanquin up the two-thousand-foot climb to the temple of Palitana in Bhavnagar District to take part in the Mahavir Jayanti festival. Held in the Hindu month spanning March and April, this festival is dedicated to the twenty-fourth Jain Tirthankara, or perfect soul—a saint who has attained total cosmic consciousness.

Historically villages in Rajasthan were built defensively, incorporating strong stone walls when possible to act as barriers against attack. Although inhabitants are no longer in danger of a siege, houses are still built in the traditional manner within protective compounds, and fields retain vestiges of walls originally raised to protect local crops. (near Nagda, Udaipur District)

RAJASTHAN

For the last millennium Rajasthan has been politically and culturally dominated by Rajputs. Rajput honor is so highly esteemed that it is held up as worthy of emulation by the entire area. Rajput marital traditions encourage hypergamy, the custom of taking as a bride a woman from a lower social rank. This practice has aided in the broad dissemination of their culture throughout the region. Though not the largest group in Rajasthan today, they still own the majority of land, governing and farming in countless "Rajput villages." In many ways they bear a striking resemblance to the Kshatriyas, members of an ancient Vedic caste who were the traditional ruling and military aristocracy of India. Rajputs are superb military leaders; as a group they will dedicate their lives for a cause they believe in, and their legends abound with stories of sacrifices made in defense of their honor. Although most Rajputs today are simple farmers, all identify with this chivalric image. They are strong-tempered, resourceful, inflexible in their integrity, sure of their superiority, and ready to fight for their rights.

Communities have traditionally been built with defense in mind: homes have flat roofs and strong outer walls made of mud-packed rock. Rajput families prefer to have separate dwellings for their women, who are carefully protected and are still kept in strict seclusion in many villages. In poorer households, several related men and boys will live in one house, but each man will maintain another house, where his wife, mother, unmarried sisters, and young children live. A Rajput woman's life is focused on her courtyard, which is usually in the center of the building she occupies and is surrounded by adjoining rooms. She is rarely seen in public and then must cover her face with her veil, but in the close cluster of Rajput houses she may visit a friend's house by crossing over the flat roofs. A village man will have temporary access to his wife's courtyard at night, but must return later to sleep in the men's quarters. A rural Rajput's self-esteem is derived from his lands, which ideally he would prefer not to work himself. In practice, however, poorer Rajputs farm industriously and are often tenants trying to raise the necessary capital to purchase their own lands. Even so, their social position within the community is exalted and they tend to be paternal in their dealings with local occupational and laboring castes.

Rajasthan's roughly square shape is divided down the center by the Aravalli Mountain Range. Its southeastern half, which is rocky, hilly, and relatively fertile, supports crops of wheat, millets, and maize, and is riddled with Rajput towns and villages. Prior to independence this area contained nineteen princely states, all of which were characterized by constant warfare and shifting populations. Rajasthan's northwestern half (the size of Virginia) is covered by the great Indian desert, the Thar. The area's ten inches of annual rainfall and its temperatures in excess of 115 degrees Fahrenheit during the summer months have understandably made it less desirable for habitation than the southeast, and as a consequence it was divided into only three Rajput states. Those who farm in the desert cultivate large acreage for meager returns; the rest subsist by herding animals, or through craftsmanship and trade. Throughout Rajasthan the monsoon rains which blow north from the Arabian Sea are usually deflected by the winds coming southeast from the Iranian plateau. As there are no major rivers in the state, droughts are frequent and aid is often required from the central government. Thirty-eight million people live in Rajasthan, but because of the harsh conditions existing there, population density is extremely low—194 people per square mile throughout most of the state and less than 50 per square mile in the desert regions. Rajputs have customarily held education in low regard. At independence this state had less than a five percent literacy rate. Since that time, although efforts have been made to redress the situation and considerable progress has resulted (the figure now stands at twenty-four percent), Rajasthan's literacy rate is still the second lowest in the country.

Rajasthanis excel in artistic endeavors, and crafts have developed into one of the few means of generating income in this harsh, infertile land. The numerous small Rajput kingdoms competed with one another to see who could create the most beautiful fortress cities, and as a result the rural craftsmen within their realms were generously supported. To offset the muted tones of the landscape, villagers dress in brilliant colors and paint the walls of their houses with vibrant frescoes. With the dissolution of the princely states, however, lack of patronage plunged many rural craftsmen into poverty. The recent demands of tourists and foreign markets for the traditional crafts of Rajasthan —block-printed and tie-dyed textiles, chased

and damascened brass, lacquered furniture, enamel jewelry, and paintings on cloth and paper—have led to a resurgence in craft activity and production. In addition to these items, for which Rajasthan is justifiably famous, products which were originally made solely for local village consumption (simple metalware, pottery, terracottas, woolen cloth, heavy silver jewelry, woodcarvings, toys, and dolls) are being made by cottage industries for sale in Indian cities and even abroad.

The economy and lifestyles of Rajasthan's desert people are presently undergoing substantial changes. The discovery of massive water reserves underneath the Thar Desert has generated the building of India's largest irrigation canal system, funded by the central government and the World Bank. Within the past few years hundreds of miles of canals surfaced with stone have been built in the desert. Some are now functioning, and others will soon be completed, opening up thousands of square miles of cultivatable land to Indian farmers. The area which has historically been India's most forbidding is now its new frontier. The effect this will have upon the settled and migratory peoples of the region can only be surmised. These desert folk, who in desperation smear the stone faces of their holy images with cow dung to taunt the gods into sending them rain, will have the very foundations of their ancient cultures shaken. The newly arable lands will also undoubtedly attract massive immigration from overpopulated areas. The result will be yet another synthesis of peoples and customs, a contemporary example of the age-old Indian process of rural adaptation and assimilation.

Throughout Indian history Rajputs have been celebrated for their skill as equestrian warriors, and good horsemanship is still considered a noble talent. A fresco painted by a Chitera (a member of the artisan caste) on the wall of a Rajput house in Bundi District depicts a family hero and serves to establish the superior caste identity of the homeowner.

A *pagri,* or turban, identifies a man's caste and community.
Plain, block-printed, or tie-dyed, the color and pattern of the
fabric (often twenty yards long) and the intricate way in which it
is wrapped vary from region to region.

Annual crops of wheat and vegetables make the mountainous
region surrounding the Aravalli Mountain Range Rajasthan's
most self-sufficient. Wheat is still harvested in the ancient
manner with short sickles, the grain beaten from stalks under
bullocks' hoofs and then winnowed by hand in the wind.

In the fertile region of Udaipur District in the Aravalli Mountain
Range, water is more plentiful than elsewhere in Rajasthan. Even
so, Rajput women must still travel some distance from their
homes for household water, while water used in irrigation is
drawn from wells using pots secured to wheels turned by
bullocks. (near Nagda)

Nomads continue to roam Rajasthan's deserts and mountains as they have for thousands of years. Here, a woman leads a camel, which carries a wooden bedstead (*charpoy*) and her toddler son. (Bikaner District)

Dancers at a wedding in Ajmer District display the traditional garments of Rajasthani women. Their skirts, called *ghagras,* are very full, sometimes requiring as much as twenty yards of material. *Odhanis*, or veils, cover their heads and hang to the length of the skirt behind. Modesty demands that they be drawn over the face and bodice when the wearer is in the presence of strangers.

Each fall tens of thousands of village Rajputs travel by foot, camel, horse, bullock cart, train, and bus to Pushkar Lake in Ajmer District for a large fair (*mela*). The desert surrounding the lake becomes a sea of tents, people, and animals. Rajasthanis come to the sacred lake dedicated to Brahma to wash away their sins and to the *mela* to buy and sell camels and to compete in or watch camel races and Rajput games of strength and agility.

Folk dances and puppetry performed by itinerant artists are a major source of rural entertainment in Rajasthan. Wooden marionettes carved in the likenesses of epic and Rajput heroes enact favorite village stories at weddings, festivals, and fairs.

The long wool warp of a Chamar's loom extends into the court-yard, where it is tied to a post. The weaver squats in a narrow pit below the loom, creating the weft by passing his shuttles from hand to hand through the warp threads. (Som, Jaisalmer District)

In the middle of a street tufts of natural cotton are quilted between two layers of cloth to make a bedcover. (Bundi District)

Nothing is wasted in Indian villages. When a wedding or festival *sari* is worn out, the gold or silver brocaded borders are cut off and burnt to separate out the precious metal, which can then be sold. The cloth from the rest of the *sari* is used to make quilts or appliqués.

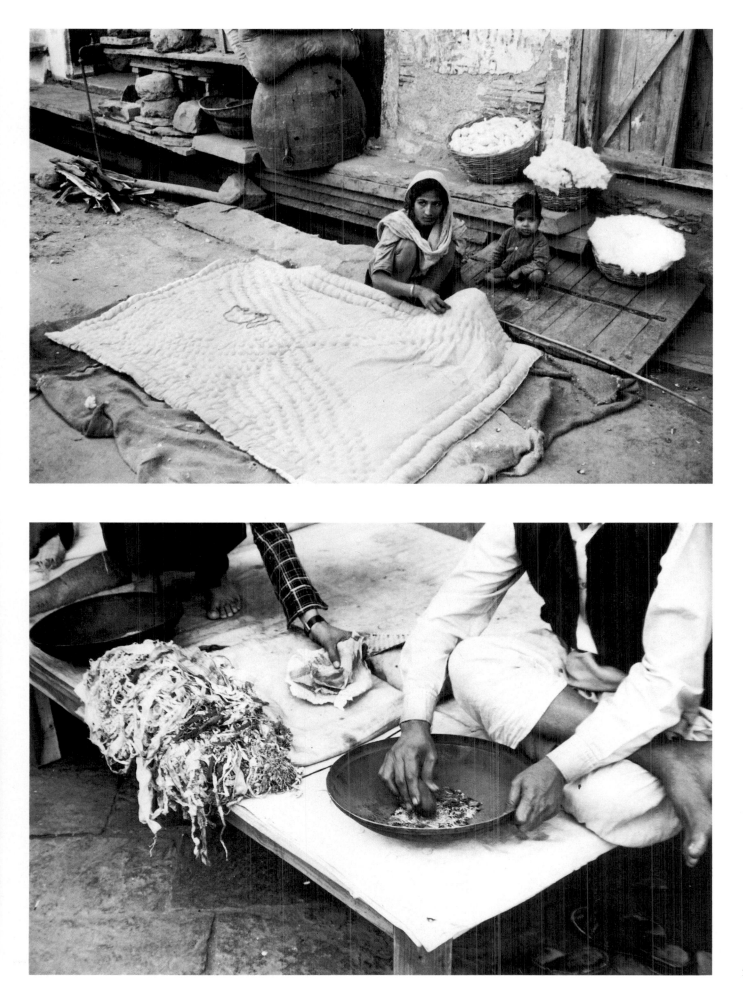

EPILOGUE

The Vale of Kashmir's sheltered position between mountains and its extremely fertile soil provide ideal growing conditions, and some of India's finest crops are raised here. In early spring mustard and crocuses (from which saffron is made) are already blooming in some terraced fields while fruit trees flower in the foreground. Villagers will await warmer weather before planting other fields with rice and oilseeds.

Flowers of innumerable species abound in Kashmir. They are grown commercially on small farms, such as this one, for export throughout India and for use in perfumes and scented oils.

KASHMIR

Kashmir is unlike any other area of the world. It is set apart by its geography, its peoples, its cultures, and its products. It is politically part of the Republic of India, yet the laws governing it are unique. As South Asia's most valuable land, Kashmir has been sought after and fought over for centuries and is still an area of prime contention between India and the countries on its borders. Kashmir's position in a book on Indian villages is also something of an anomaly. Separated by more than four hundred miles from the northernmost villages discussed in this text, the peoples and cultures of rural Kashmir are dissimilar and not comparable to those of mainland India. Kashmir is presented here as it stands within the subcontinent: distinct and unusual, a point of beauty and of contrast.

The Vale of Kashmir is an oval, eighty-four miles long and twenty to twenty-five miles wide, wedged between gigantic Himalayan mountains. This valley is the focus of the state, the center of centuries of attention, the area of greatest population and productivity, and hence the primary subject of this section. It comprises Srinagar District in the central western part of the state of Jammu and Kashmir, which is roughly the size of Illinois and has a population of only 6,700,000—the third lowest in India. The state of Jammu and Kashmir is an amalgamation of two previously separate kingdoms. (Subsequent references to the state apply to this whole area; references to Kashmir indicate the Vale.) Although located farther north than any other region of India, more so even than Tibet, the latitude of

Kashmir is the same as that of South Carolina. The floor of the valley lies at an average altitude of 5,400 feet. The mountains immediately surrounding it rise to eighteen thousand feet and behind them some of the world's highest mountains tower well over twenty-six thousand feet. Kashmir, unlike most of India, has four seasons: harsh, snow-bound winters, abundant springs, hot summers, and cool autumns. The encircling mountains feed its valley with innumerable streams, creeks, and rivers, which bring with them a rich alluvial soil that, combined with an idyllic climate for three seasons, provides ideal conditions for growing flowers, fruits, and vegetables.

Kashmir has traditionally been South Asia's link with Central Asia and the Far East. Through it pass twenty-six ancient routes and gateways to India, formerly the means of passage for conquerors and for trade. Kashmir was a pivotal point along the old Asian Silk Route, through which the wealth, products, and knowledge of ancient India were transmitted to Asia. It also gave access to the numerous invasions of Huns and Central Asians that so changed the course of India's history. For most of its existence Kashmir has been ruled by foreigners. The leader Ashoka in the third century B.C. converted its original inhabitants to Buddhism, and Kashmiri missionaries were the first to introduce that religion into Central and Eastern Asia. A Hindu heyday followed in the seventh and eighth centuries A.D., when arts were patronized and Kashmir indulged in a rare period of territorial expansion. Islam did not take root in Kashmir until relatively late, in the fourteenth century, but its initial rule there was enlightened and its effect enormous (to this day most Kashmiris are Muslim). By the time the Mughals seized power in the late sixteenth century, Kashmiri borders had long been open to Afghanistan, Persia, and the Middle East, and the strong cultural influence of these countries can still be discerned in many of the region's contemporary crafts. Kashmir was at the heart of Mughal aspirations. Throughout the reign of this dynasty the Mughals moved their courts from Agra or Delhi to Kashmir during the hot season. There they built fabulous gardens, installed intricate irrigation systems (still in use today), and eulogized the Vale in paintings, poetry, and songs. In the early eighteenth century, after the ruler Aurangzeb's death, control was wrested from the Mughals by the Afghans, who were, in turn, supplanted by the Sikhs. The English gained control in 1846 and gave to the Dogra, the hereditary maharaja of Jammu (a Hindu), the leadership of Kashmir. Kashmir's importance to the British derived from three factors: its strategically vital geographic position between the Soviets and the Chinese (a position which is still tactically critical to Indian policies); its economic importance as a source for both manufactured goods and produce; and its desirability as a retreat from the hot Indian summers. Kashmir's maharajas, all of whom were Jammu Dogras, ruled under the British until independence in 1947. Since that time the state has been a constant source of dispute between nations, particularly between India and Pakistan. Three wars have been fought over its sovereignty. As things stand now the Vale and most of the original state are under India's jurisdiction; a quarter of the state's

territory in the extreme west, called Azad Kashmir, is under Pakistan's rule; and the borders of a section in the far northeast are under dispute by India and China.

Kashmir's varied racial and cultural history is reflected in the faces of its people. The broad extremes of Mongolian and Sino-Tibetan features can be seen side by side with the light hair and blue or green eyes of Middle Eastern Muslims. The Muslim population of the state of Jammu and Kashmir is seventy percent, while that of the Vale is ninety-three percent. Of the remaining seven percent, five percent are Hindu, 1.8 percent Sikh, and the balance primarily Christian and Buddhist. The massive influx of Hindu tourists to the Vale during the summer months, although aiding the economy, adds to a general Hindu-Muslim antipathy, and occasional rancorous outbreaks occur. Jammu and Kashmir has no tribal peoples, and in the state only eight percent are listed as Harijans. Centuries of close political and business associations with Mughals and Persians have resulted in the emergence of numerous proud Muslim families. Many Hindus are also counted among Kashmir's elite. They are Brahmans, locally referred to as Pandits, and most of them live in the capital city of Srinagar. (The family of Jawaharlal Nehru, his daughter Indira Gandhi, and his grandson Rajiv Gandhi are Kashmiri Pandits.) Kashmiri Muslims are divided into castes such as overlords, merchants, farmers, oil pressers, potters, carpenters, fishermen, barbers, servants, and sweepers. The upper classes are educated, but, as a whole, the state has India's lowest literacy rate (18.3 percent). Kashmir is eighty-

one percent rural, and apart from Srinagar and the few towns that exist, people live in isolated homesteads, aboard boats, and in scattered tiny hamlets. Although the valley is rich in craft production and agriculture, and Kashmiri exports are in demand all over India and abroad, rural homes are often poor and insubstantial. The standard of living is rising slowly, however.

The basis of the rural economy in Kashmir is divided between revenue from farms and forestry and from cottage industries. The orchards here grow India's finest apples as well as peaches, pears, pomegranates, and walnuts. Mulberry, crocus, and mustard plantations provide silk cocoons, saffron, and mustard. Rice, oilseeds, and vegetables are also grown. Pine, fir, and cedar as well as walnut wood are primary exports. The tourist industry and a constant demand for trade goods support the over 150,000 craftsmen in Kashmir. The products of these workers are supplemented by those of farmers, shepherds, and foresters who turn to craftsmanship to provide them with their livelihood during the long winters. The majority of craftsmen are involved in textile production. Kashmir's long history as a focal point for trade has engendered superb artistry unexcelled elsewhere in India. Kashmir was most famous for its intricately woven and embroidered woolen shawls, which for centuries were a cornerstone of European fashion until the invention of the Jacquard loom enabled the production of less expensive Paisley shawls. Thirty thousand workers, many of them rural, still weave and embroider Kashmiri shawls, which remain a status symbol in India. Another forty thousand weavers produce hand-woven fabrics. This prodigious output has made Kashmir one of India's leading regions in the production of handloom textiles. In addition, craftsmen employing techniques learned from Persia centuries ago man over three thousand carpet looms and are capable of tying silk and woolen carpets whose quality rivals those of the Middle East. The Vale of Kashmir is also famous for many other cottage industries, among them the making of papier-mâché, the carving of walnut, and the production of wickerwork. Besides manufacturing goods, Kashmiris are known throughout India for their mercantile skills. The combination of the superb artistry of simple Kashmiri villagers and the consummate international marketing ability of Kashmiri businessmen may help to improve the rural economy, bringing about an increase in the people's standard of living. If this happens, the valley's extraordinary natural beauty will be matched by economic prosperity as well.

Left: In the floor of the Vale houses are larger, often built of wood and brick or stone. In a community where water traffic is integral to business, houses are placed as close as possible to the water's edge.

Below: Long wooden barges called *doongas* transport wood and produce up and down Kashmir's rivers. Many villagers live in small huts constructed of wood and straw on the decks of their *doongas*.

Opposite, above: Small communities of wooden houseboats, the homes of farmers, fishermen, servants, and laborers, line the canals and rivers. Much larger houseboats in Srinagar cater to tourists.

Opposite, below: Village girls have paddled their slender boats out into the center of a lake to gather lotus greens for cattle fodder.

259

Waterways are the focus for much of village life. Here, a Kashmiri woman washes her cooking pots and pans at the river's edge. She is wearing the traditional female Kashmiri costume of baggy pyjamas, voluminous tunic *(kangri)*, and head scarf. In winter she will strap a basket of coals beneath her *kangri* to keep herself warm.

Two men wrapped in shawls moor their small boat, called a
shikara, alongside a riverbank to make afternoon tea.

A Dhobi (washerman) washes embroidered woolen shawls in a canal before they are taken to the city to be sold. Most are made out of sheep's wool *(pashmina)*. The most valuable shawls, called *shatoosh*, are made from the beard hairs of the wild ibex and are so fine that a whole shawl can be pulled through a small finger ring.

Waiting for the shawls to dry the Dhobi and his wife squat beside a tobacco hookah and a tea samovar—the traditional accoutrements of relaxation in India.

Many village shops open right out onto the water to provide easy access for boats. Merchants travel in *shikaras* laden with goods for sale. Here, shawls, embroideries, metalworks, and wood carvings are displayed for the tourist market.

Apple blossoms in a small orchard provide a backdrop for a villager who is saying his midday prayers while facing Mecca.

BIBLIOGRAPHY

Allchin, Bridget and Raymond. *The Rise of Civilization in India and Pakistan*. Cambridge: Cambridge University Press, 1982.

Anand, Mulk Raj, ed. "Bihar Handicrafts." *Marg*, vol. 20, no. 1. Bombay: Marg Publications, 1966.

———, ed. *In Praise of Aihole, Badami, Mahakuta, Pattadakal*. Bombay: Marg Publications.

———, ed. "In Praise of Tamil Nadu Heritage." *Marg*, vol. 33, no. 2. Bombay: Marg Publications, 1980.

———, ed. *Splendours of Tamil Nadu*. Bombay: Marg Publications, 1980.

———, ed. "Terracottas." *Marg*, vol. 23, no. 1. Bombay: Marg Publications, 1969.

Annandale, N. "Plant and Animal Designs in the Mural Decoration of an Uriya Village." *Memoirs of the Asiatic Society of Bengal*, vol. 11, no. 1. Calcutta: Asiatic Society of Bengal, 1929.

Bahadur, K. P. *Caste, Tribe and Culture of India: Andhra Pradesh, Madhya Pradesh, and Maharashtra*. Delhi: Ess Ess Publications, 1977.

———. *Caste, Tribe and Culture of India: Bengal, Bihar, and Orissa*. Delhi: Ess Ess Publications, 1977.

Barrett, Ken, and Suresh Sharma, eds. *The Indian Experience*. Bangkok: Media Transasia, 1982.

Basham, A. L. *The Wonder that Was India*. New York: Taplinger, 1968.

Beals, Alan R. *Gopalpur: A South Indian Village*. New York: Holt, Rinehart and Winston, 1962.

Bernardi, Debra, Lisa Marrongelli, and Tom Szentgyorgyi, eds. *Fodor's India, Nepal, and Sri Lanka*. New York: Fodor's Travel Guides, 1984.

Bernier, Ronald M. *Temple Arts of Kerala*. New Delhi: S. Chand and Co., 1982.

Berreman, Gerald D. *Hindus of the Himalayas: Ethnology and Change*. Berkeley: University of California Press, 1972.

Bhardwaj, Surinder Mohan. *Hindu Places of Pilgrimage in India*. Berkeley: University of California Press, 1983.

Bhat, H. R. Raghunath. "Some Terracotta Images from North Kanara." *Archaeological Studies*, vol. 1. Mysore, India: University of Mysore, 1976.

Briggs, G. W. *The Chamars*. Delhi: B. R. Publishing Corp., 1975.

Chattopadhyaya, Kamaladevi. *Tribalism in India*. New Delhi: Vikas Publishing House, 1978.

Critchfield, Richard. *Villages*. New York: Anchor Press/Doubleday, 1983.

Crooke, William. *Religion and Folklore of Northern India*. London: Oxford University Press, 1926.

Dalip, D., ed. *Terracotta*. Madras: Craft Council of India, 1981.

Dalton, Edward Tuite. *Tribal History of Eastern India*. Delhi: Cosmo Publications, 1973.

Danielou, Alain. *Hindu Polytheism*. New York: Bollingen Foundation, Pantheon Books, 1964.

Das, J. K. *The Tribes of Orissa: A Census of India Publication, 1961*. Cuttack, Orissa: Government of India Press, 1972.

Das, K. B., and L. K. Mahapatra. *Folklore of Orissa*. New Delhi: National Book Trust, India, 1979.

de Schweinitz, Karl. *The Rise and Fall of British India: Imperialism as Inequality*. London: Methuen, 1983.

Doshi, Dr. Saryu, ed. "Heritage of Karnataka." *Marg*, vol. 35, no. 1. Bombay: Marg Publications.

Doshi, Dr. Saryu, Dr. Jan Pieper, and Dr. George Michell. *The Impulse to Adorn: Studies in Traditional Indian Architecture*. Bombay: Marg Publications, 1982.

Dube, S. C. *Indian Village*. New York: Harper and Row, 1967.

Durrans, Brian, and Robert Knox. *India: Past into Present*. London: The British Museum, 1982.

Dye, Joseph M. *Ways to Shiva*. Philadelphia: Philadelphia Museum of Art, 1980.

Elson, Vickie C. *Dowries From Kutch: A Women's Folk Art Tradition in India*. Los Angeles: Museum of Cultural History, University of California, 1979.

Elwin, Verrier. *The Tribal Art of Middle India*. London: Oxford University Press, 1951.

Eschmann, Anncharlott, Hermann Kulke, and Gaya Charan Tripathi. *The Cult of Jagannath and the Regional Tradition of Orissa*. New Delhi: South Asia Institute, 1978.

Fabri, Charles. *History of the Art of Orissa*. New Delhi: Orient Longman, 1974.

Farmer, B. H. *An Introduction to South Asia*. London: Methuen, 1983.

Fischer, Eberhard, Sitakant Mahapatra, and Dinanath Pathy, eds. *Orissa: Kunst und Kultur in Nordost-Indien*. Zurich: Museum Rietberg, 1980.

Fischer, Eberhard, and Haku Shah. *Rural Craftsmen and Their Work: Equipment and Techniques in the Mer Village of Ratadi in Saurashtra, India*. Ahmedabad, India: National Institute of Design, 1970.

Fuchs, Stephen. *The Aboriginal Tribes of India*. London: The Macmillan Press, 1977.

Gandhi, Indira, and Jean-Louis Nou. *Eternal India*. New Delhi: B. I. Publications, 1980.

Government of India. *Census of India, 1981.* New Delhi: Government of India Press, 1982.

Gray, Basil. *The Arts of India.* Oxford: Phaidon Press, 1981.

Hacker, Katherine F., and Krista Jensen Turnbull. *Courtyard, Bazaar, Temple: Traditions of Textile Expression in India.* Seattle: University of Washington Press, 1982.

Handa, O. C. *Pahari Folk Art.* Bombay: D. B. Taraporevala Sons, 1975.

Hobson, Sarah. *Family Web.* Chicago: Academy Chicago, 1982.

Hunter, W. W. *Annals of Rural Bengal.* Delhi: Cosmo Publications, 1975.

Jain, Jyotindra. *Folk Art and Culture of Gujarat.* Ahmedabad, India: The Shreyas Folk Museum, 1980.

Jayakar, Pupul. *The Earthen Drum: An Introduction to the Ritual Arts of Rural India.* New Delhi: National Museum, 1980.

Kramrisch, Dr. Stella. *Unknown India: Ritual Art in Tribe and Village.* Philadelphia: Philadelphia Museum of Art, 1968.

Kramrisch, Dr. Stella, Dr. J. H. Cousins, and R. Vasudeva Poduval. *The Arts and Crafts of Kerala.* Cochin, India: Paico Publishing House, 1970.

Leslie, Charles, ed. *Anthropology of Folk Religion.* New York: Vintage Books, 1960.

Maloney, Clarence. *Peoples of South Asia.* New York: Holt, Rinehart and Winston, 1974.

Marriot, McKim. *Village India: Studies in the Little Community.* Chicago: The University of Chicago Press, 1972.

Maury, Curt. *Folk Origins of Indian Art.* New York: Columbia University Press, 1969.

McNeil, William H., and Jean W. Sedlar, eds. *Classical India.* New York: Oxford University Press, 1969.

Miller, Barbara Stoler. *Exploring India's Sacred Art: Selected Writings of Stella Kramrisch.* Philadelphia: University of Pennsylvania Press, 1983.

Mitchell, A. G. *Hindu Gods and Goddesses.* London: Her Majesty's Stationery Office, 1982.

Mohanti, Prafulla. *My Village, My Life, Nanpur: A Portrait of an Indian Village.* London: Corgi Books, 1973.

Mohanty, Gopinath. "Fading Outlines in Tribal Culture." *Adibasi, 1963-64,* no. 3. Bhubaneshwar, Orissa: Harijan and Tribal Research cum Training Institute, January 1964.

Moraes, Frank, and Edward Howe, eds. *India.* New Delhi: Vikas Publishing, 1974.

Nagaswami, R. *Art and Culture of Tamil Nadu.* Delhi: Sundeep Prakashan, 1980.

Pal, M. K. *Crafts and Craftsmen in Traditional India.* New Delhi: Kanak Publications, 1978.

Pirie, P. *Kashmir: The Land of Streams and Solitudes.* London: John Lane, The Bodley Head, 1909.

Rawlinson, H. G. *India: A Short Cultural History.* New York: Frederick A. Praeger, 1968.

Russell, R. V., and Hira Lal. *Tribes and Castes of the Central Provinces of India.* 4 vols. Delhi: Rajdhani Book Center, 1975.

Saraf, D. N. *Indian Crafts: Development and Potential.* New Delhi: Vikas Publishing, 1982.

Saskena, Jogendra. *Art of Rajasthan: Henna and Floor Decorations.* Delhi: Sundeep Prakashan, 1979.

Schwartzberg, Joseph E., ed. *A Historical Atlas of South Asia.* Chicago: The University of Chicago Press, 1978.

Senapati, Nilamani, and Nabin Kumar Sahu, eds. *Gazetteer of India: Orissa: Koraput District.* New Delhi: Government of India Press, 1966.

Sharma, Brijendra Nath. *Festivals of India.* New Delhi: Abhinav Publications, 1978.

Shashi, Dr. S. S. *The Shepherds of India.* Delhi: Sundeep Prakashan, 1978.

Singh, Raghubir. *Kashmir: Garden of the Himalayas.* New York: Thames and Hudson, 1983.

Skelton, Robert, and Mark Francis. *Arts of Bengal: The Heritage of Bangladesh and Eastern India.* London: Whitechapel Gallery, 1979.

Spear, Percival. *A History of India.* vol. 2. Middlesex, England: Penguin Books, 1982.

Stutley, Margaret and James. *A Dictionary of Hinduism: Its Mythology, Folklore and Development, 1500 B.C.–A.D. 1500.* London: Routledge and Kegan Paul, 1977.

Thapar, Romesh, ed. *Tribe, Caste, and Religion in India.* Meerut, India: The Macmillan Company of India Limited, 1977.

Thapar, Romila. *A History of India.* vol. 1. Middlesex, England: Penguin Books, 1972.

Tiwari, A. N., Mohapatra N. Sahoo, Monoranjan Das, and Gourikumar Brahma, eds. *Third Purba Bharat Sanskritik Sammelan.* Bhubaneshwar, Orissa: Government of Orissa Press, 1976.

Tyler, Stephen A. *India: An Anthropological Perspective.* Pacific Palisades, California: Goodyear Publishing, 1973.

Vidyarthi, L. P., and B. K. Rai. *The Tribal Culture of India.* Delhi: Concept Publishing, 1977.

von Furer-Haimendorf, Christoph and Elisabeth. *The Gonds of Andhra Pradesh: Tradition and Change in an Indian Tribe.* London: George Allen and Unwin, 1979.

von Niggermeyer, Hermann. *Kuttia Kond: Dschungel-Bauern in Orissa.* Verlag Klaus Renner, 1964.

Wacziarg, Francis, and Aman Nath. *Rajasthan: The Painted Walls of Shekavati.* New Delhi: Vikas Publishing House, 1982.

Wallbank, T. Walter. *A Short History of India and Pakistan from Ancient Times to the Present.* New York: Mentor Books, 1965.

Watt, Sir George. *Indian Art at Delhi, 1903.* London: John Murray, 1904.

Watts, Neville A. *The Half-Clad Tribals of Eastern India.* Bombay: Orient Longmans, 1970.

Weir, Shelagh, ed. *The Gonds of Central India.* London: The British Museum, 1973.

Younghusband, Sir Francis. *Kashmir.* New Delhi: Sagar Publications, 1970.

Zaehner, R. C. *Hinduism.* London: Oxford University Press, 1972.

INDEX

All numbers in this index refer to page numbers; those in italic type indicate illustrations.

PHOTOGRAPH CREDITS